MAKING
SMALL GROUPS
WORK

Resources by Henry Cloud and John Townsend

Boundaries
Boundaries Workbook
Boundaries audio
Boundaries video curriculum
Boundaries in Dating
Boundaries in Dating Workbook
Boundaries in Dating audio
Boundaries in Dating curriculum
Boundaries in Marriage
Boundaries in Marriage Workbook
Boundaries in Marriage audio
Boundaries in Marriage curriculum
Boundaries with Kids
Boundaries with Kids Workbook
Boundaries with Kids audio
Boundaries with Kids curriculum
Boundaries with Teens (*Townsend*)
Boundaries with Teens audio (*Townsend*)
Changes That Heal *(Cloud)*
Changes That Heal Workbook *(Cloud)*
Changes That Heal audio *(Cloud)*
Hiding from Love *(Townsend)*
How People Grow
How People Grow Workbook
How People Grow audio
How to Have That Difficult Conversation You've Been Avoiding
Making Small Groups Work
Making Small Groups Work audio
The Mom Factor
The Mom Factor Workbook
Raising Great Kids
Raising Great Kids for Parents of Preschoolers curriculum
Raising Great Kids Workbook for Parents of Preschoolers
Raising Great Kids Workbook for Parents of School-Age Children
Raising Great Kids Workbook for Parents of Teenagers
Raising Great Kids Audio
Safe People
Safe People Workbook
12 "Christian" Beliefs That Can Drive You Crazy

DR. HENRY
CLOUD &
DR. JOHN
TOWNSEND

MAKING
SMALL GROUPS
WORK

What Every Small Group Leader
Needs to Know

ZONDERVAN.com/
AUTHORTRACKER
follow your favorite authors

ZONDERVAN®

Making Small Groups Work
Copyright © 2003 by Henry Cloud and John Townsend

This title is also available as a Zondervan audio product.
Visit www.zondervan.com/audiopages for more information.

Requests for information should be addressed to:

Zondervan, *Grand Rapids, Michigan 49530*

Library of Congress Cataloging-in-Publication Data

Cloud, Henry.
    Making small groups work : what every small group leader needs to know / Henry
Cloud and John Townsend.
        p. cm.
    ISBN-10: 0-310-25028-5
    ISBN-13: 978-0-310-25028-9
    1. Church group work.   2. Christian leadership.   3. Small groups—Religious
aspects—Christianity.   I. Townsend, John Sims, 1952–   II. Title.
BV652.2.C572003
253'.7—dc21

                                                                                    2003011380

Published in association with Yates and Yates, LLP, Literary Agent, Orange, CA.

Interior design by Tracey Moran

Printed in the United States of America

07 08 09 10 11 12 13 14 15 • 20 19 18 17 16 15

This book is dedicated to
small group leaders everywhere.
May God richly bless your efforts
to help your group discover more
about him, life, themselves,
and each other.

Contents

PART 1

HOW SMALL GROUPS HELP PEOPLE GROW

PART 2

WHAT HAPPENS IN A GOOD GROUP

PART 3
STARTING A SMALL GROUP

PART 4

THE RESPONSIBILITIES
OF GROUP FACILITATORS

PART 5

THE RESPONSIBILITIES
OF GROUP MEMBERS

PART 6

How to Deal with
Problems in Groups

Acknowledgments

Sealy Yates, our agent, for helping to guide our writing lives through the years. Your wisdom and discernment have been a welcome help to us, and we thank God that you are in our lives.

Scott Bolinder, our publisher, for your commitment to quality publishing. Your concern for the value of the written word to the church has helped many over the years.

Sandra Vander Zicht, our editor, for your many hours of work on this book, and your friendship. We have appreciated your careful attention to our books in order that the ideas may be as accessible as possible to readers. Thanks also to editors Joan Huyser-Honig and Jim Ruark for helping us to say more clearly and succinctly what we are so passionate about communicating.

The staff at Cloud-Townsend Resources for their sacrificial and tireless efforts over the years to multiply and enrich small groups throughout the world. Your work has certainly helped launch many groups for the first time and improve the lives of many others. Maureen, Kevin, Jody, Raul, Kris, Belinda, thank you.

Mariner's Church and Jim Gaffney for your help over the years to give a great "lab" to our materials and small group vision over the years. May God continue to bless the fruits of all you are doing there.

Dr. Phil Sutherland, for your training in the power of the small group to change and heal. Your input helped us to understand the power and the complexity of the small group process, and we ask God's blessings on how you influence others.

The staff of the former Minirth-Meier Clinic West hospital programs for your competence and care in using small groups. Many years ago your partnership with us helped a great deal of people in small groups in many profound ways.

Thanks and appreciation from Henry to the staff of Answers for Life also for your vision and work to create and enhance the evangelistic and growth mission of small groups throughout the country. Your sacrifice is a model to all who have a passion for this kind of work. Denis and Marianne, Scott and Claire, Robbie and Terri, Lillie, Steve and Colleen, and Becky, thank you.

Henry would like to thank Willow Creek Community Church and the Willow Creek Association for allowing me to be a part of your efforts to equip small group leaders around the world. It has been inspiring to work with you over the years, and I appreciate all that you do to help the church realize that small groups are more than an "add-on" to church, or a fad. You have helped many to see that what occurs in small groups is not just something "at the church." It is church. Thanks to Rex, Bill, Russ, Kristen, Katherine, and Stephanie.

Henry would like to say thanks to my pals at CCN for helping to get small group training broadcast to churches all over America. It has been a lot of fun, and I look forward to many times of broadcasting the concepts in this book. You are awesome to work with: Bill, Ryan, Deb, Jay, Peter, and all.

Henry and John would like to thank their own small groups over the years for helping them to grow. We are different because of you.

Tapping into the Power of Small Groups

Astrong wind is blowing across the church, and it is good. More and more churches are starting small group ministries. Some small groups meet for fellowship and support. Others meet to address specific life topics such as marriage, parenting, dating, addictions, or divorce recovery. Still others gather to study the Bible or to grow spiritually or even to engage in spiritual formation.

One truth that has emerged from this small group movement is that *there is no one right way to do small groups.* Just as there are many mansions in God's house, so there are many different needs in God's body, the church, and today we are much more able to find a group somewhere that is designed to meet those needs.

God has placed many different gifts in his people to meet those needs. Indeed, we are a Body. In his grand design we exercise those gifts with each other and help each other grow. The small group is one of the best ways for this to happen. So it is no surprise that churches are rushing headlong into the small group movement.

Also, the local church has varying degrees of commitment to a small group program. For some, it is an add-on program, an option, or a part of what they offer. For others, the groups are integrated with the church's mission and designed to deepen the life past what happens in a weekly service. For still others, the small group is not a *part* of what they do, it *is* what they do.

But no matter what the style, topic, or emphasis, most churches or ministries that do small groups encounter two common challenges: *how do we get leaders,* and, *once we have them, how do we train them?* In a sense, these two are almost the same, for the biggest barrier to someone volunteering to lead a small group is often his or her feeling of "not knowing how."

That brings us to the topic of this book. For the past twenty years we have been involved with small groups of various kinds, some in professional clinical settings, parachurch ministries, and churches, and some in less formal settings such as homes, workplaces, and other settings. Through participating in small groups, leading them, training their leaders, consulting for them, and researching them, we have come to believe that the small group is without a doubt one of the most powerful tools of life change and spiritual growth.

But *not all small groups experience that life-giving power.* Many groups lack the life-changing spiritual and relational growth members hunger for. As a result, members lose interest, and the small group ministry does not grow and does not achieve the vision with which it began. *This does not have to happen.* Leaders can learn skills and biblical processes that make small groups more effective. That's why we wrote this book.

As we wrote this book, we had in our minds and hearts four groups of people:

1. The pastor or overseer of small groups who needs a simple tool to train his or her small group leaders
2. The person who desires to lead a small group but needs to know how

3. The members of those groups who desire deep life change
4. The people in the lives of group members who can be reached as a result of the members having had a good experience

Small groups are so powerful, and the skills required to lead a small group so learnable, that a lack of "know-how" does not need to stand in the way.

As we talked to church and other ministry leaders, we found that they were well trained in the structural aspects of small group ministry, such as how to launch, cast a vision for, and design a small group ministry, but they needed more practical, hands-on guidance for the leader. Over and over they would ask us the following questions: How can I get my leaders ready to lead? How can I equip them?

If you put yourself in the shoes of small group leaders, you can quickly see that while they might have good curriculum that guides the content and structures the path of the group experience, they need training in *the process itself*: "Once I sit down with eight people in my living room on Thursday evening," . . .

"How do I create safety?"
"What do I do if someone talks too much or dominates the group?"
"What do I do if no one talks?"
"How do I decide if someone is 'too needy' for the group?"
"How do I confront someone? Should I?"
"Should the group give feedback to each other?"
"What do I do with strong emotions?"
"How do I know I am succeeding?"
"How do I know whether God is pleased?"
"What are my real responsibility and role as a leader?"
"Where does my role end and the members' begin? How are they different?"

The list of realities small group leaders face is virtually endless. The good news is that they can learn answers to their questions and uncover principles to allay their fears. This is how we designed this book. We do not emphasize the big picture of small group ministry, although we do begin with a theological vision for small groups and a large view of what we believe small groups do. Instead, we focus on what pastors and overseers need for their small group leaders and on what those leaders tell us they need the most: "Show me how to do it. Tell me how to create a small group process that works." We designed this book with one end in mind: *how do you do small groups that change lives?*

We have witnessed the power the body of Christ wields in the small group setting: "From him the whole body, joined and held together by every supporting ligament, grows and builds itself up in love, as each part does its work" (Ephesians 4:16).

We have seen members of Christ's body grow in truly amazing ways, past what we thought possible, when "all the parts" were doing their "work." We believe wholeheartedly in the power of small groups, and every day we receive letters and testimonials from people who enter into the process with fear and trembling, but come out with new life.

Being the instrument God uses to connect people to himself and to his life is exciting. And not knowing how to lead a small group does not need to stand in the way any more than having only a few fish and a few loaves of bread stood in the way of the original leaders' goal of feeding a large crowd of people.

It's okay to be afraid, for the task can seem overwhelming. We have all been there. But it is doable, and chances are someone has already thought you could do it or you wouldn't be reading this book! All you need is a few tools. So join us as we take a look at the "how-tos" you need to make your small group work, and we look forward to the results! God bless.

Henry Cloud, Ph.D.
John Townsend, Ph.D.
Newport Beach, CA

PART 1

HOW SMALL GROUPS HELP PEOPLE GROW

Chapter 1

God's Surprising Plan for Growth

I will never forget the scene. I (Henry) was doing a training session with seventy-five ministry leaders on how to build small groups that change lives, and they were getting excited about the possibilities. On that particular afternoon I talked about the psychological and relational healing that people experience as they open up with others in a small group. I told of miracles I had seen, and I tried to cast a vision of how life-changing their ministries could be if they learned a few simple concepts.

Then it happened. A guy in the middle of the room just couldn't take it anymore, and he erupted. "I can't allow this to go on any longer!" he said.

"Allow what?" I asked, somewhat taken aback by his interruption.

"This distortion of the Bible," he said. "I can't allow it."

I asked what he meant by "distortion of the Bible." God knows, that is the last thing I would ever want to do, so I wanted to hear him out.

"People grow in one way—through teaching the Bible, preaching the Word of God!" he said. "All this stuff about vulnerability and opening up to each other in groups is not in the Bible. You are distorting the way people grow. We are to teach the Word and let the Bible do its work."

"Well," I said. "Let's see what the Bible itself has to say. Let's see, for example, what Paul thought about 'opening up' to each other." You could feel the tension in the room.

I opened my Bible and read: "We have spoken freely to you, Corinthians, and opened wide our hearts to you. We are not withholding our affection from you, but you are withholding yours from us. As a fair exchange—I speak as to my children—open wide your hearts also" (2 Corinthians 6:11–13).

I went on to read other passages that affirmed the basic power of community and relationships and the New Testament's commands for us to walk in community. I gave an apologetic for how the body of Christ helps us grow. But the man was not buying in so quickly. Instead, he gave me a lesson from his own experience.

"I grew by learning the Bible and walking in the Spirit," he said. "My life changed by learning that one truth. Then when I learned more about the Bible, my life continued to change. I was radically transformed by the Truth. Before that, I was a mess. I was out of control, and a lot was wrong. God changed my life by that one truth."

I know the ministry he was involved in when this all happened. I also know enough about life change to describe what I thought had happened.

"I am sure that learning the Bible and walking in the Spirit were *huge* for you, as they are for all of us in the spiritual life," I said. "I cannot imagine trying to grow or change without those two things. But I also know enough about the ministry you were in to know that other things happened as well.

"You were a college student, floating and lost. You were, as you say, 'out of control.' Then a leader from the ministry reached out and in very real ways befriended you. He told you about God. He taught you some of the truths you are talking about.

"Then he did something else that was key. He invited you to become part of a small group of students that he led. Together you studied the Bible and learned God's transforming truths. But you did much more.

"You also, in that small group, *lived out and experienced those truths.* You opened up to each other about your struggles. You confessed your sins to each other. They offered and helped you feel God's forgiveness. You held each other accountable. When you went through tough times with school or your girlfriend broke up with you, the group supported you, cried with you, and helped you sort it out. They prayed with you, and you sought God together.

"Next they recognized your talents and abilities and encouraged you to use them. They challenged you to take risks, to grow and stretch. In fact, you are probably here today because they pushed you out of your comfort zone more than once.

"When you failed, they comforted you, but did not let you quit. You grew because they encouraged you as your family never did.

"Also, they modeled how to do life. They showed you how to relate and accomplish things in ministry. They let you watch how they did it and then try it for yourself. In that process, you became a lot of who you are today.

"As that community did studies on relationships, you confessed how you fell short in your dating life and you began to treat others differently, starting with them. You learned how to give acceptance and be honest with others—confronting them when necessary, holding them accountable, and being more real than you had ever been.

"I could go on about your involvement with that community and small group, but I think we get the picture. You are right when you say your life was radically transformed. And you are right when you say that God's truth and learning to walk in the Spirit changed your life. But you are wrong when you say that all growth, even your own, comes only from 'teaching and preaching' or learning the Bible. For that is not what the Bible says.

"Your growth also came from the role that the body of Christ, your small group and your leader, played in your life. They delivered the 'goods' you learned about in the Bible. They obeyed what it said to do, and you were the beneficiary.

"Now, the question is, why do you do one thing and say another? Why do you receive those gifts of God and yet tell others that they are to grow some other way? Why do you rob them of what you yourself have experienced and what Paul commanded the Corinthians to do?" I said.

The room was silent. Everyone was reflecting on their own experience of change through spiritual relationships and small group communities. The man I'd addressed just looked at me and then went on with some sort of "yes, but . . ." about the *real value* coming out of teaching and preaching. But he was caught, and the others knew it as well.

The "Say-Do" Gap

I did not really fault the man for his position. He had inherited it from many teachers before him. In fact, he and I met later on and had very good talks. He eventually came around to thinking we were "saying the same thing," as he put it. At least, he began to say that small groups and community are a valid part of the process. Whether or not he would say they are *as valid* as teaching was a little harder for him to do.

But I could understand where he was coming from. It was the "say-do" disconnect. Often, what we say or what we believe is not really what we do or what happens in real life, even when things go well. We say that *one* thing causes growth, when in reality we do *many things* to accomplish that growth. The say-do disconnect is common in the church.

We hold up, and rightly so, Bible study, spiritual disciplines, and direct relationship with God as the paths to spiritual formation. We talk about them, teach on them, practice them, and read books on them, and they slowly become a paradigm in and of themselves of how we grow. And they are vital.

Even so, at the same time, we are doing other things as well. We are connecting with each other, supporting each other, encouraging each other, confessing to each other, and doing a zillion other things the Bible tells us to do in community. All these produce growth, healing, and change. Yet we don't often have a theology for those actions. We do them by happenstance or because our church has decided to "get current" and have some small groups. But we don't hear much biblical teaching on how we grow through connections with other believers in a small group, at least as being a part of doctrine.

In short, while we have a cultural movement of small groups in the church, we often lack a theological vision for their role. Nor do we have practical ways of how to do that vision. We have not given small group processes the weight the New Testament does. As a result, we often experience a stagnated, limited version of being in relationship with God. If by chance we do experience growth through groups, we don't recognize God's role in it. Without a theological vision for growth through small groups, we lose it.

I felt for the man and his limited view that all God does comes through the Bible or direct intervention. I felt also for the people under his teaching. But I was not judging him—because I used to share his view. I had to learn the hard way how God uses small groups and community.

Plan A and Plan B

I went to college with big dreams and expectations. When I was a high school senior, the Southern Methodist University golf coach invited me to Dallas to tour the school and recruit me to come play golf there in the fall. I remember the excitement of playing a U.S. Open course on that trip and dreaming about playing college golf. One week before I left for college, a tendon popped in my left hand. The severe pain abated with cortisone treatments, but it would come back as soon as the medicine wore off. When I got to school, the coach who had recruited me had left, and I was never pain-free long enough to build on my skills. Finally, after two years of struggle, playing well for a while and then poorly, I quit the game that I had dedicated my youth to.

Feeling depressed and bored with my studies, I tried to keep my lost feelings at bay with parties and dating.

One day I was in my dorm room obsessing about my empty life. I could not make the ache go away.

Then something happened that would forever change my life. I looked up on my bookshelf and saw my Bible—the one I had not read since coming to college. I remember thinking, "Maybe something in there would help." So I opened it, and a random verse jumped out at me: "But seek first his kingdom and his righteousness, and all these things will be given to you as well" (Matthew 6:33).

I read it again. "What things?" I asked myself. Then I looked at the whole passage. It was telling me to seek God first and then all these things that I was obsessing about would fall into place.

Was that really true? Was there really a God who could do that? And if he really were there, would he? My thoughts raced as I considered God in a way I never had before. I wasn't just "thinking about God." I was being presented with a defining choice.

I decided to go for it. Sensing the seriousness, I walked across campus and looked for a church. Alone in a dark, empty chapel, I looked up and told God that if he were really there, I would do whatever he told me to do. If he would just show up, I would follow him and do what he said. I waited for him to "zap" me. I waited for a vision. Nothing happened.

I remember feeling a great sense of both relief and emptiness. Relief because after years of playing around with God, I'd come clean and said I would give it all. But empty because I did not sense him there and knew that if he did not show up, I was alone in the universe with nowhere to go and no way to find my way. Doing it on my own had not gotten me very far. I just stared at the ceiling, still wanting him to zap me. Finally I walked back, cold and dreary, to my room.

A while later, the phone rang. It was a fraternity brother. We hadn't talked recently, but he was calling to invite me to a Bible study. I remember his saying that it was strange that he even thought to call me, as I was not overtly into spiritual things. But he felt moved to do it—and I felt as if God was maybe showing up just as I had asked.

Maybe I would go to this Bible study and find God. I thought someone might pray for me, or I would pray, and then God would reach down and finally zap me supernaturally. I would be healed. I would feel good again. I'd find answers to all I was supposed to do. A princess would fall from the sky. After all, I was going the "God route" now, and I expected a miracle.

Well, I did not get my zapping. But I met some new people. Bill, a seminary student, led the Bible study. He and his wife, Julie, opened up their home to me. I decided to take a semester off from school to figure it all out. I moved in with them, and they and another small group became my new spiritual community.

Still depressed and lost, I asked Bill why God did not zap me and make me feel better. His answer—one several people had given as I'd opened up about my feelings—was an answer I was beginning to hate. He said, "Well, sometimes God does that, and he just heals people. But *God uses people, too."* That was the phrase I hated: *"God uses people, too."*

Bill meant that I had a lot to learn, and he wanted me to "get discipled" and learn about the faith. He also wanted me to get counseling for my depression, another way God uses people. And he thought I should be involved in more spiritual community and relationships. I remember thinking that "God uses people, too" was a "Plan B."

To me, if you were going to get something from God, you should get it "from him," not from people. That was my Plan A—the real spiritual healing, the miracle cure. I thought that when we pray and ask God to heal or to change our lives, he should zap us with a supernatural something. Lightning, earthquakes, visions, or something like that. Knock me down and fix me.

This "God uses people" seemed a spiritual cop-out. If God did not do something, then people had to. So how was that really God? Even if it were God, it was somehow less than the real thing, the zap. But, since I was getting no zapping, I didn't have much of a choice. I got involved in all the small group experiences Bill suggested.

Over the next months, people in my groups loved me, corrected me, confronted me, challenged me, taught me, supported me, and helped heal deep pain and loss. They forgave, accepted, and pushed me. I was learning that I was emotionally disconnected and lacked key relational skills, even though I had a lot of friends. I was not as "real" as I thought I had been. My small group friends taught me that my performance and accomplishments provided a flimsy foundation for measuring my life and my acceptance.

My life was changing through being in a small group, as when the sun comes up in the morning. You don't know exactly when daylight occurs. But you know when it has arrived and that it happened through a process.

One morning I woke and thought, *I am not depressed anymore.* Lying in bed, I pondered how full life had become. I had purpose, meaning, and a new set of talents and abilities the group had encouraged me to pursue. I had new friends and lots of experiences with God. The Bible had become my love. I studied it all the time, and I was having more fun dating than I had without God. Imagine that! All in all, I thought, life is good again. No, not again. In many ways, for the first time. I was full in a way I never had been. And I knew I had God to thank for giving me this new life and all these people who had helped me. I also had another thought, which seems silly now, but gets to the heart of what happened that day I was training those ministers: *I feel good, but I still wish God had healed me. He never did.*

I still thought I had gotten Plan B. In my thinking, the supernatural zap was Plan A, and "God uses people, too" was Plan B. I was healed, but God didn't do it, at least not directly. He did it through people. It was like going to the Super Bowl but sitting in the cheap seats. I saw the game, but not from the box. I got the healing, but not directly from him. I got second best. Still, I was grateful and moved on.

Then one day something happened to further change my life and my understanding of how people grow. I was reading in Ephesians about how we grow into maturity: "From him the whole body, joined and held together by every supporting ligament, grows and builds itself up in love, as each part does its work" (Ephesians 4:16).

I read the verse again. A few thoughts struck me. *From him*, meaning God, *the body*, meaning us, *grows*, meaning changes, as *each part does its work*, meaning that people help each other. That was *exactly* what I had experienced in my own life and what I had seen while working with others. And this passage said it was *from him* that *the body* does these things. It hit me in a new way. What I had called Plan B, God using people, was not a cop-out at all. It was really God's Plan A. He had written right there in the Bible that he planned for his people to grow through people helping people. The body would "build itself up in love." God had healed me after all! Not in some secondary way, but in the way he had intended from the beginning. It was not the cheap seats! This was the fifty-yard line!

Then I began to see this truth all over the pages of the New Testament. God was saying the same thing in many different places: "Each one should use whatever gift he has received to serve others, faithfully administering God's grace in its various forms. If anyone speaks, he should do it as one speaking the very words of God" (1 Peter 4:10–11).

While I had been waiting for God to zap me supernaturally, he had been doing just that. He was zapping me with the love he had put into those around me. He was zapping me with truthful confrontations from those in my group. He was zapping me with healing as they held my hurts and pain. God had been working in the way he designed his body to work—and *it worked*. And that was Plan A all along.

A New Vision

So why do we begin a book on small groups with that lesson? For the same reason I had to have that discussion in the training room of ministers that day. And for the same reason I myself was lost for a long time, thinking that if God was not "zapping" me supernaturally with lightning bolts, then he was not zapping me at all. (By they way, he did do some supernatural zapping as well, just to let you know I believe in that.) We begin with this lesson because so many of us need it and so many of the churches in which you will be leading small groups need it as well.

As we have stated, Paul said the body has work to do if we are going to grow. It is work that only partly happens in a big cathedral-like room on a Sunday morning. Much of that work can't happen in a big room with a lot of people at once. Much of it has to happen in a smaller setting, a more intimate, safer one. One of the best places for this work to happen is in a small group.

What I said earlier is very important. We need to *elevate* the small group process to more than just a "keeping up with the times" way of doing church. Many churches start small group ministries because they see that the churches that are growing have them; they are following the leaders. Many others do it because someone in the church carries the torch for it. Others do it for "special concerns" like recovery or divorce or other areas of focus where people need help.

But no matter why anyone does small groups, one thing should be clear. *Small groups are not an add-on, secondary concern, or fad. What happens in a good small group is part of the very work of the church itself. It is primary, and should be seen that way.* For what you are about to embark on, whether or not your church leadership feels the same way, hold your head high and know that God is very much for the process of his people getting together to help each other grow. It is part of Plan A.

So we want to begin with a new vision for small groups. They are not just culturally relevant for the postmodern world of reality and experienced truth. They are not just a way to be like the "cool" churches. They are not just for the "hurting" people. And they are not just an add-on program. They are a valid expression of what the body of Christ is supposed to be doing on the earth. They are a structured expression of the doctrine of the church. They are as big a part of what the New Testament dictates as preaching and teaching.

So begin there with the knowledge that all of New Testament theology is on your side. God is on your side if you are doing the things in your small group that he tells us to do. And if done well, your church and community are going to be on your side, too, because lives are going to be changed. That is the vision we hope you get for your church, for your leaders, for the people who attend your groups. It is a vision of realizing the total message of the New Testament, one person at a time, one group at a time.

A New Vision with Many Applications

Have you ever known longtime Christians who have significant areas that are not changing? Or they relate to others in ways that are real problems? Have you ever wondered how someone like that can go to church for that many years and not change? What about the person who reads the Bible and knows it better than most, but you can't stand to be around him? What is going on there?

All of us have seen that happen. Most of us have also been that person at one time or another. But what is going on is often no mystery and can be solved. We see the miracle of change over and over again. Once you understand it, things become clear.

What often happens is that someone has been in the faith, doing the disciplines, or attending church, *but has still not been involved in some of the life-changing processes the New Testament commands us to do.* As a result, sometimes change cannot be forthcoming, even with sincere people. But we have seen something else.

Many times these people have never had these New Testament processes offered to them. They have never seen them in practice and have never been taught them. But the Bible is very clear about our need for them. *And, then, when people who have been stuck find themselves involved in a small group that is actually doing the things the Bible says to do in that context, life change occurs that has never before occurred.* That is what we want you to see as well as you embark on the fulfilling role of leading a small group of people further into the realities of life change that God has designed.

You might have a group on basic doctrine or parenting or marriage or recovery from addiction. There are many different kinds of groups. You might be doing a seeker-oriented group designed to introduce people to the things of God for the first time. Or a divorce recovery group or an accountability or prayer group. There are many different applications of the small group process. Our vision is that no matter what kind of group you are doing, certain processes are life changing, and when you implement them to varying degrees, you will see healing and change you never thought possible.

It is to that end we have designed this curriculum. No matter what kind of group you are leading, we think that you can be an instrument of life change for the people who are a part of it. And we don't think that it takes a Ph.D. to do that! We think it takes some basic skills and processes found in the Bible, plus a little dose of love, a mustard seed of faith, some commitment, and an adventuresome spirit. If you have those qualities, you probably have what it takes to facilitate a group that can do what Paul talked about. The group can be an instrument God uses to help others "grow up" in him (Ephesians 4:15). They can learn about God, become better parents, date in more healthy ways, overcome addictions and other recovery issues, heal marriages, and on and on. All because you got a new vision—that God's Plan A is to use you and others to help each other grow.

Chapter 2

What Are We Trying to Do as Small Group Leaders?

W hen you were asked to be a small group leader, what were you thinking? Did you agree to do it and shake in your boots afterward? Or do you feel confident, knowing exactly what you want to accomplish as you lead others down a path of growth?

Chances are you might be somewhere in between. Small group leaders often desire to serve, especially after experiencing a good small group themselves, yet may feel lost about what to do. Some console themselves, "Oh, it's not that big a deal. I just have to find the time and place, bring the snacks, and the materials will do the rest." Or they may say, "It isn't my job to teach; that is the pastor's job. I am just a facilitator." Others feel enormous pressure to make sure each person in the group experiences the benefits that the group title promises. For example, you might feel it is up to you that your group members recover from divorce, grow spiritually, or develop a strong marriage. Do you feel up to that? Have you had the training you need to take on this weighty responsibility?

Certainly anyone would feel weak-kneed if, with little training, he or she accepted responsibility to "make" all those things happen. In reality, even people who do those things for a living have limited control to change other people's lives. But you are a leader now, and you're expected to make some things happen. Don't panic, though. We'll help you be clear about your role. Leading a small group can be very rewarding, and simplifying your role will help you lead with confidence.

A Common Cause

Each group has its own agenda and goals. The agenda can range from general spiritual growth to specific topics such as marriage, recovery, divorce, dating, parenting, or discipleship. Or you may be part of a neighborhood Bible study group to study the Scriptures, have meaningful prayer, and support one another.

If you are a layperson leading a group with specific goals and content, you have most likely been provided with or have secured appropriate materials. If your coach or leader has done his homework, he has found a structure designed by someone who has reached that goal before you, and your job is to facilitate that path. Your program or curriculum should guide you *in terms of content.* If not, see the appendix of this book for help in selecting materials for your group.

But what about goals *that relate to process, not content?* Which transcendent goals and tasks apply to each and every group, no matter what its purpose or topic? Are there some bottom-line goals to help you know you are being helpful?

Here's an analogy. If you're a parent trying to help your child with math, how might you recognize and measure success, apart from content? One answer might be, "Well, I tried to help my kid with math, and I don't know if I succeeded, but at least he knows that I love him and am there for him." In other words, we're saying that regardless of the group's specific task, *there are transcendent purposes to which you can anchor yourself—and thus accomplish good in any group.* You can *know,* no matter what else happens, that you accomplished some good things.

Living in a Fallen World

Every member in any group experiences the common problem of living in a fallen world. As fallen people, we love and deal with other fallen people. Because Adam and Eve passed on to us the art of going our own way, we all encounter fallen spiritual, relational, psychological, emotional, and functional dynamics. *If you address and facilitate growth within these dynamics, you will help people, no matter what kind of group you lead.*

These dynamics started in the Garden of Eden. Adam and Eve had a good relationship, were healthy, and loved their work—until something happened. They tried to take God's place. As a result, life as it was created to be lived became unavailable. *In their attempt to become godlike, they lost their ability to be fully human.* What did that mean for Adam and Eve, and what does it mean for your group?

Disconnection from the Source of life. God had provided all they needed for life—materially, relationally, spiritually, and in every other way. When they decided to play his role, humankind fell into trying to provide for itself independent of God. We went down the path of trying to be self-made.

Dual loss of relationship. Adam and Eve lost their relationship with God, and they became alienated from each other. Their intimacy with him and one another was replaced by fear, hiding, mistrust, and other things that your group members know too well.

Shame. Adam and Eve felt ashamed, judged, and condemned. To cope with guilt, they began to perform and, worse, to hide who they really were. They covered their vulnerability with fig leaves, just as we become false to look better than we are.

Disobedience. Humankind lost God's authority in our lives and no longer naturally obeyed him. We became our own bosses, going our own way, and disobeying his ways, to our loss. It is a *Home Alone* scenario with an outcome of disastrous pain and injury.

Lost knowledge of God's ways. With little knowledge of God's ways, we disregard learning what he says. God designed life to work in very specific ways. He has told us how to relate to one another, set and reach worthwhile goals, and get through difficulties. But we try to figure it out for ourselves without consulting the designer or the manual.

Lost control. God was originally in control of everything except us. He left us free to control ourselves but intended that we yield the rest of the universe to his control. We were to trust and to yield. When we fell, we reversed course. We lost control of ourselves (self-control) and began trying to play God and controlling everything else around us, especially other people. So we no longer feel in control of our own lives and try to control everyone and everything around us.

Your Ministry of Reconciliation

This is where your group comes in. Instead of giving empty religious answers to these problems, you have another calling. God has not called you to be moral police who set people straight. *He has called you to help restore life unto himself in the way it was created to be.* The Bible's word for this is *reconciliation.* God's purpose is to reconcile things back to himself and to *use you in that process.* As Paul says:

> All this is from God, who reconciled us to himself through Christ and gave us the ministry of reconciliation: that God was reconciling the world to himself in Christ, not counting men's sins against them. And he has committed to us the message of reconciliation. We are therefore Christ's ambassadors, as though God were making his appeal through us (2 Corinthians 5:18–20).

No matter whether your group's purpose is support, Bible study, or recovery, the transcendent goal is the *ministry of reconciliation.* You are bringing people back to God and the life he created for them to live. Now you have the incredible and *very realizable* call to help your group members:

- *Reconnect to the Source* of life and see that God is the source of whatever they are trying to accomplish in life and in the group
- *Reconnect through real relationship* to God and through experiencing connections with others within the group

- *Experience total grace,* acceptance, and forgiveness in the group—and the absence of shame, guilt, judgment, and condemnation
- *Learn and experience the value of obedience to God* as the authority of life
- *Learn God's ways* and how to apply them to life situations
- *Give control to God* for the rest of life (and relax in doing so) but take control and responsibility for themselves

Celebrate this: You can help your group achieve these six universal aspects of reconciliation *while you pursue your group's specific goals.* You will reverse the effects of the Fall in their lives and bring about lasting change as you implement the foundations of the gospel into their everyday experience.

What Reconciliation Looks Like

Becoming a leader seems complicated. That is why we start by emphasizing the simple but profound elements of redemption possible in every group. Through creativity, seeking, and prayer you will find countless ways to live out these six points of spiritual growth. The following examples sketch only a partial model of how a specific content group, such as a parenting group, can help members transcend the topic and be reconciled to the life of God. In other words, no matter what the topic, you can help by remembering the six points stated above.

Return to the Source. Group members are taught or discover that they can turn to God moment by moment for help in tough parenting situations. They learn that God will provide answers, strength, community, opportunities, and everything they need to be a parent. They will experience God's provision through:

- Prayer
- Orienting parenting around turning to God for answers
- Leaning on God for strength
- Sharing testimonies with each other about how they bring God to parenting

- Becoming prayer partners through the week for their parenting

Reconnect. Group members learn to reconnect in real relationship with God and other parents. They learn to tell God about their struggles, share their victories, draw strength from daily relationship with him—and realize, maybe for the first time, that they're not going through parenting alone. Also, they learn to share with and lean on each other. They find that God uses group members to deliver support, answers, wisdom, encouragement, correction, modeling, strength, and comfort. This reconnection happens as the group experience:

- Teaches them to walk through the parenting day with God
- Teaches them to open up and share with each other their parenting lives
- Helps them share parenting needs with the group
- Facilitates mutual support and encouragement
- Helps them connect through vulnerability
- Fosters feedback for one another

Experience grace. As they learn to share failures, fears, pain, and problems and just be seen as the parents they really are, group members find they are more alike than different. They feel less judged. This frees them to take off the fig leaves and show their real selves. As grace is offered from the leader and the group, their shame, guilt, and condemnation lessen. As time goes on, they internalize the group's acceptance and learn to accept themselves. They treat their failures as opportunities to learn instead of toxic opportunities to feel guilty, ashamed, or "less-than." They experience grace as they:

- Confess their parenting failures to the group
- Confess their parenting failures to God
- Confess their parenting fears and pains to the group
- Give grace and forgiveness to each other
- Model total acceptance in the group for parenting failures and inadequacies

Renew obedience. Group members get encouraged to obey God, follow him as the authority for life, and develop structured, fruitful obedience. Some for the first time see others seek to do what God asks and find a new way of life. They find in the context of community the benefits of living life the way he says. The group experience:

- Facilitates an orientation toward following and obeying God as a parent
- Facilitates sharing how they obey and what it is like
- Facilitates open sharing of their struggles to obey
- Holds up obedience as a life value, not some religious dogma
- Models grace despite struggle and failure

Learn new ways. Group members learn new principles and ways for living they could not have discovered on their own. They find that the Bible is the source of God's truth for living life and learn to celebrate having a "lamp to [their] feet" (Psalm 119:105). In finding truth they are relieved of the uncertainty of trying to figure it out on their own. They discover that God's ways work in the parenting arena. This learning takes place as group leaders:

- Select good and practical materials that show God's design for parenting
- Show that whether or not they are overtly Christian, the materials reflect parenting truth designed by God
- Choose quality materials that are effective in their lives, thus confirming that God has designed ways to live and parent
- Appropriately show connections between the Bible and the truth they are learning

Understand control. In learning to give up control of what they cannot control, they learn to take responsibility and control of themselves. They find out, for example, that they cannot make their children make the right choices or always keep them safe and out of trouble. But parents can control how they react, how they discipline, what they provide, and how they allow their children to influence their feelings. Parents reconcile their approach to proper control through groups that:

- Have a "serenity prayer" culture regarding parenting—to accept what they cannot change, change what they can, and seek wisdom to know the difference
- Encourage trust in God for what they cannot control or change
- Pray for the aspects of their parenting situation they cannot change or control
- Focus on what they can do and help the group discover from each other and the materials what they can control and change in their parenting
- Impart this aspect of reconciliation to their children as well, teaching them to develop self-control and responsibility as "big picture" items of spiritual growth
- Hold each other accountable for being responsible and taking control of themselves in their parenting life, feelings, attitudes, and behaviors

These simple concepts comprise much of the essence of Christian growth and discipleship. And they apply to every group, not just parenting.

Preparing for Your Exciting Journey

We are excited for you as a small group leader. You have embarked on one of the most incredible journeys available to us as Christians. You are in a position to help people not only study your particular group topic but also see the big picture of getting life back to the way it was created to be. It is simple, but profound, and we believe you can do it.

We have found it most rewarding to help people grow through the small groups we lead in our work, and we want the same for you. Once you understand a few basic concepts and develop a few basic skills, the results can be incredible. Every day we get feedback from all over the world that as these principles are implemented, lives change. People are healed, families reconciled, dreams realized.

We began this chapter acknowledging that small group leaders sometimes feel afraid, knowing they are shepherds responsible for the sheep in their groups. James says, "We who teach will be judged more strictly" (3:1). Although a small group leader is not necessarily a "teacher" in that regard, the principle applies to some degree.

Don't let this scare you off! You have probably just signed up to be a facilitator, not a judge, teacher, elder, or pastor. You might be thinking, "Wait a minute! I never said I knew enough to do this." Don't resign just yet.

Neither we, the Bible, nor (hopefully) whoever talked you into leading a group will hold you to an impossible standard of perfection. No one thinks you have to have it all together. But here is an important principle about achieving transcendent goals through small group dynamics: *The more you possess something, the more you can give it away.*

It's worth examining yourself daily to see how you're doing in these six areas of spiritual growth. None of us is perfect, and as James says in the next verse, "We all stumble in many ways" (3:2). Jesus reminds us to find and remove obstacles to our spiritual growth:

> Why do you look at the speck of sawdust in your brother's eye and pay no attention to the plank in your own eye? How can you say to your brother, "Brother, let me take the speck out of your eye," when you yourself fail to see the plank in your own eye? You hypocrite, first take the plank out of your eye, and then you will see clearly to remove the speck from your brother's eye (Luke 6:41–42).

The more we practice the six aspects of reconciliation in our own lives, the more we will understand them and be able to impart them, creatively and naturally, to others. Even a very young Christian could be on the path of these six. They are matters of the heart, not knowledge. Look at them again:

- See God as the source of life and all we need.

- See relationship as our primary need in life, with him and other people.
- Seek and practice grace and forgiveness.
- Submit to God as the boss.
- Seek his ways to live.
- Let God be in control of the world and others; develop control of oneself.

None of these tasks presumes that if you are leading a group on whatever topic, you will know everything about that topic. As we have said, good materials provide much of the content and knowledge. These six concepts constitute a basic orientation toward God, people, and growth that everyone can grasp as they turn to him. That is why we are excited about these principles. You can embrace them, and when you do, they can be "caught" by others. That's how this "ministry of reconciliation" (2 Corinthians 5:18–20) has been passed on for two thousand years. One person catches it and becomes God's ambassador to another. We think you can do that as well.

We have to humble ourselves in our own growth process first and keep practicing. *Not perfectly, but faithfully.* Remember, the Bible shows that God uses *faithful* people, not perfect people. If you faithfully practice these areas, God will make you fruitful. You will become a source of spiritual growth for others without even knowing how "the seed sprouts and grows" (Mark 4:27).

Chapter 3

The Ingredients of Grace, Truth, and Time

Your group's ultimate purpose is a ministry of reconciliation. Achieving this purpose requires three ingredients: grace, truth, and time. Your first challenge may be to help your group understand that grace and truth are far richer concepts than many Christians realize; we will describe how the Bible teaches them so that you can make them the foundational aspects of your group. Your second challenge may be to help your group take the long view. The ingredients of grace and truth don't yield immediate growth. They need time to work.

Whether or not your group starts out knowing they need grace, truth, and time, they'll probably feel a desire for "more of something" than they have now. Some of us know what "doing better" would look like—and know we are not there yet. Others of us aren't even sure of the standard. But most groups will start with these experiences in common:

- We are aware that there is something "better" than where we are.
- We know we are failing at varying levels.
- Our failures cause feelings of guilt, shame, condemnation, and inferiority.
- We desire better.
- We feel powerless to get there on our own.

Paul says it like this:

We know that the law is spiritual; but I am unspiritual, sold as a slave to sin. I do not understand what I do. For what I want to do I do not do, but what I hate I do. And if I do what I do not want to do, I agree that the law is good. As it is, it is no longer I myself who do it, but it is sin living in me. I know that nothing good lives in me, that is, in my sinful nature. For I have the desire to do what is good, but I cannot carry it out. For what I do is not the good I want to do; no, the evil I do not want to do—this I keep on doing. . . . So I find this law at work: When I want to do good, evil is right there with me (Romans 7:14–21).

A few verses later Paul tells how to be delivered from the law—a delivery you will become part of. "What a wretched man I am! Who will rescue me from this body of death? Thanks be to God—through Jesus Christ our Lord!" (Romans 7:24–25).

You will bring your group members an experience of being rescued by Jesus from the wretchedness Paul describes. You will help rescue them from knowing they need to grow but being unable to do it on their own. You will give them the real God, the one who is both Grace and Truth and who uses time as a redemptive season to change us.

Grace and Truth: Growth Requires Both

If you are familiar with other books we have written, you may already know that we define grace as far more than forgiveness. It is *unmerited favor*. We define truth as *God's truth, the reality that structures our lives*. The next few pages will give you a fuller understanding of the rich concepts of grace and truth. But we want to alert you to these definitions so you understand what follows.

Giving and Receiving Unmerited Favor

Too often, Christians understand grace only as forgiveness or unconditional acceptance or the absence of condemnation. Certainly those are aspects of God's grace, but grace is more than that. It is God's giving to us what we cannot provide for ourselves. Grace is unmerited favor. It is God's bestowing on us good things that we do nothing to gain, earn, merit, or—and here is a big key for groups—*produce*. In other words, *grace is brought to us, not created or produced by us.* We cannot merit it.

A small group offers a powerful expression of grace in contrast with the individual spiritual walk. Other people can give us expressions of God's grace that we cannot produce for ourselves. In a good small group, *people get from others things that they are unable to give or get for themselves.*

Without this full-orbed understanding of grace, small groups fall short. They provide safety but not other aspects of grace that help people grow. In the book *How People Grow,* I (Henry) described one man's experience of truncated grace. Dangerously overweight, this man learned from his doctor that he needed to lose more than a hundred pounds. He came up with a program of diet and exercise and formed an accountability relationship with my friend.

My friend continued to meet with him during the weight loss regimen, but the man's weight went up, not down. My friend wondered what to do. So I asked about their program. They had a plan with goals and tasks, such as monitoring food and exercising. The man was to pray and study the Bible as well. But the main plan was to stick to these goals.

Then he would meet with my friend for an "accountability" relationship. They'd get together, and he'd confess his failure. He'd feel guilty and repent, receive forgiveness, and commit to doing better. The "deeper commitment" language seemed to be a big part of the plan. This overweight man and my friend had decided that he just needed to commit to more self-discipline.

When my friend asked me what to do about the failure, I responded that the plan lacked grace and was destined to failure. Caught off guard, my friend said, "No. I give him a lot of grace. We pray, receive God's forgiveness, and I accept him, too. He has total grace." I knew my friend was right about that, because he is a very accepting and gracious person. But the program itself was falling short of grace. *It had forgiveness but was missing "unmerited favor."*

To experience victory, the man needed the whole of grace. In other words, he needed unmerited favors. He needed people from the outside to give what he was not able to produce for himself. Where is someone without self-discipline going to get it? From himself? We just said he did not have any, so it can't be from himself. It has to come from outside. Otherwise, it would be like telling a car that is out of gas to "get more self-gas" or "get more committed." If it could have kept running on empty, it would have. Grace is the gas pump that comes alongside the car and gives it what it needs to make the trip. It is the rescue that Paul mentioned in Romans 7. The overweight man had to join a group that could give him more than forgiveness and acceptance. Such a group could provide:

- Safety to lovingly let him know that he is powerless to get there on his own
- Acceptance and love in his powerlessness, just the way he is
- Forgiveness, such as he was already getting
- Support and encouragement to reach the goal
- Help through weakness, such as group members he could call when tempted to eat or skip exercise
- Healing of the pain and grief that he was covering up with food
- Support in stressful situations that he was "eating over"
- People to give honest feedback on his plan and progress
- A place to process his failure and learn why and how he fails
- Limit-setting and confrontation on his other excesses
- A push to see that their group was not enough and that he also had to join a more structured program

Do you see how through the group the man could receive *gifts from the outside?* Asked to provide those disciplinary things for himself, he could not do so. He needed unmerited favor—good things that he could not produce. That is why they are grace. And the more your group sees grace that way, the more people will grow. It is a culture of asking, "What do you need that we can give you?" Then the group gives what is needed or supports the person to go out and seek it.

Again, don't get overwhelmed. You don't have to figure out the right kind of grace for every problem. Your group's particular materials and content aids should do that for you. Instead, you must make sure that the individuals see grace as more than forgiveness and get good things from others in the group. That's true facilitation—not doing everything yourself, but making sure it happens through the group.

Seeing Ourselves in Relation to God's Truth

Remember my experience with the minister who stood up and protested my talk about how people need other people to help them grow? He was adamant that people grow in response to "the truth." He thought that God's truth was what made people grow. But he limited that definition. He thought that truth is delivered only through preaching and teaching. He believed that if the pulpit does its job, everyone will complete the growth process.

We agree that truth is an important element in growth. If we do not have God's truth, we do not know how to live. As Moses said, "The LORD commanded us to obey all these decrees and to fear the LORD our God, so that we might always prosper and be kept alive, as is the case today" (Deuteronomy 6:24). David prayed, "Show me your ways, O LORD, teach me your paths; guide me in your truth and teach me, for you are God my Savior, and my hope is in you all day long" (Psalm 25:4–5).

But the Bible also teaches many ways of *realizing* God's truth. Along with seeing the truth of his statutes, we also have to see the truth of who we are in relation to those standards. We have to see how to grow toward those statutes. Teaching and preaching help us grow, but so do other experiences. We need all these aspects of truth at work in our lives, and a small group is a great context. Here is a partial list of how groups help us grow in truth:

- Teaching—instruction of God's truth
- Confessing—telling the truth about where we are (James 5:16)
- Opening up our hearts to deep truth (Psalm 51:6)
- Correcting each other with the truth (Ephesians 4:25; Proverbs 15:32)
- Containing each other's sin through confrontation (Matthew 18:15–19)
- Finding out the truth of our deepest parts (Psalm 139:23; Matthew 23:26; Mark 7:20–23)
- Learning to walk in God's truth and integrate it into life as we "hold to it" (John 8:31–32)
- Modeling truth for each other so we can do it for ourselves (1 Corinthians 4:16)
- Finding safety and security in the boundaries of God's truth (Proverbs 1:33)
- Hearing truth from each other in ways that build us up (1 Thessalonians 5:11)
- Helping each other build character (2 Peter 1:5–8)
- Revealing the truth of our pain so we may grieve and be healed (Romans 12:15)
- Opening up honestly so we may be more closely knitted together (Ephesians 4:15–16, 25)

This is just some of what the Bible teaches and group research affirms regarding the different ways God uses the truth in our lives. Certainly teaching is important, but do not limit your experience with the truth to one sermon a week. The small group is a place where that truth can be taught, caught, and realized in very important ways.

In fact, experiencing truth in a group would drastically affect the overweight man I described. Applying the truths listed above would create an almost perfect prescription for weight loss. Doing those things would help him much more than just dieting, being held "accountable," and then trying harder. If he were letting the truth work in these ways, the solution would be happening that would help him lose the weight he needs to lose.

Grace and Truth Dwelling among Us

Small groups must avoid two extremes: grace only or truth only. Perhaps you've found one group that loved you, accepted you, forgave you, helped you, and showed you all sorts of grace. Yet not enough change took place over the long haul, because you did not learn new ways of being or doing, or didn't get input and correction about how you were already being or doing. You weren't held accountable. And there wasn't enough probing to uncover deeper truth about what needed healing and changing. So you remained comfortable and stuck in your grace group, but not growing. You longed for more change over time.

Maybe you joined another group, a truth group, which did the opposite. You experienced direction, accountability, confrontation, structure, rules, and pressure to be different. But this group may have lacked safety and acceptance, so you felt guilty and ashamed, never good enough. You longed for more acceptance and love. The standards were strong, but the forgiveness was weak, and there were more *shoulds* than you could measure up to.

Too many people have experienced small groups that lacked something. Growth did not happen to the degree it could have, had the group mixed grace and truth. Fortunately, God had the same thought. More accurately, God *was* the thought. He himself is the combination of grace and truth, and in this combination we find healing. John puts it this way: "For the law was given through Moses; *grace* and *truth* came through Jesus Christ" (John 1:17–18).

Jesus was the realization of grace and truth together. He was total unmerited favor. He loves us, accepts us, and helps us when we don't deserve it. He favors us and brings us favors, just because he loves us. He also gives us truth—the truth of God, the truth of life and how we should live, the truth of who and how we really are. Jesus offers the love that gets us to face and deal with reality. The safety of his forgiveness and grace take the shame and sting out of our daily failure to live up to his standards.

The exciting thing about experiencing grace and truth together is that we can become friends with the standards. The way we "ought to be" can become a goal, a direction, instead of a judge. Because of grace, we can begin to say, "I want to see where I need to change, so I can be and do better. Show me the truth and where I am in relation to it." Jesus' grace enables us to become friends with truth.

Now, think as a small group leader. You are God's representative to your group. How will you help members grow? Which will you bring? Grace or Truth? Fortunately, you don't have to choose. You can bring both—you can bring Jesus, as John describes him: "The Word became flesh and made his dwelling among us. We have seen his glory, the glory of the One and Only, who came from the Father, full of grace and truth" (John 1:14).

You can bring Jesus to your group the ways that this verse describes: fleshly dwelling, glory, grace and truth. Fleshly dwelling means that God became man to live with us. God offers his gifts, love, help, and more to live inside us. We are his physical body on the earth now, dwelling with each other. As we saw in the first chapter, your group is one of the prime places where the members will be "with God."

At your meetings, God will be present—in the flesh—in grace and truth. You will help your group experience God's presence in his body— your group. They will feel God's grace through acceptance, help, love, care, support, and forgiveness. They will live God's truth through standards, accountability, principles, reality, and honest self-assessment.

As group leader, you must help make sure that the right God shows up there. In other words, you will guide processes, set the tone, and assign tasks to create a group experience in which *both grace and truth are realized.* That is who he is, the real *God.*

The rest of this book will show you how. No one gets it perfect. But if we keep the goal in mind from day one, we can get closer to it each time we meet. Remember that bringing grace and truth to your group is a process that happens over time. As the next section explains, God gave us redemptive time so he can heal and change us, gradually growing us into people more like Jesus, who perfectly and eternally embodies grace and truth.

Groups Take Time

I recently attended a party where I saw several dear friends I hadn't seen for years, not since we all worked for the same company. I had always had very warm feelings toward these folks. They were good people, and we had gotten along really well. At the party we did the usual catching up with each other's lives, relationships, and families. Later, when the lights dimmed, the music grew softer, and others left, my former colleagues and I sat around the table telling old stories. One story made me laugh so hard I couldn't breathe. Some stories were sad. Some were touching.

What struck me most about that evening, however, was how *present* those past memories were. It really seemed we were once again that group in that company again, in those former ages and stages of life. I remember looking at everyone's faces and seeing them as younger and different, the way they were then. It was a bittersweet but positive experience, a little like what the characters of the movie *The Big Chill* encountered at a reunion after their friend's death. I liked being back there with those people. And in my head, at least, for a few brief moments, *time stood still.* Things seemed just as they had been back then.

The "group experience" I just described wasn't about a growth group or support group or anything of that nature. It was just a few good friends with strong, common past experiences. Though not a group thing, it spoke to the heart of what happens in good groups: *healthy support groups provide glimpses of eternity.* That is, in a good supportive setting, daily world obligations go away for a while so growth and healing can occur. This doesn't mean that members go into denial about their real lives outside the group. It does mean, however, that groups provide people with enough time, space, and safety to deeply experience their real selves, others who care about them, and *what is truly important in life.* Today's crises, chores, and to-do lists fade from view, revealing love, loss, growth, pain, and the truth about ourselves.

Time is as necessary an ingredient as grace and truth in creating good groups. The better you understand time's relationship with group process, the better your group will be. In contrast with how easily my old friends and I talked, have you ever wanted to talk to someone about a problem or struggle but ended up talking about logistics, the daily grind, and the weather? Time intruded on your conversation, and something you might have needed was lost. So the more intentional we are with group time, the better the group operates. The more you make time your ally, the more successful your group can be.

Let's look at several principles of how time functions in groups.

Group Time Is Different from Time Out of the Group

We hope that you as a facilitator feel protective of the time you allot for your group setting. These are significant minutes in which God and the members meet face to face and conduct business. It is a different sort of time than *real-life time.* It is *redemptive time.* Let us understand a little of this term.

Time, a fairly abstract concept, refers to the measuring or passing of events: people are born; grow up; experience loves, joys, losses, and pains; find families and social contexts; find work and careers; and pass on. However, we were never originally intended by God to experience time as we know it now, something that passes us by. God lives in *eternity* and is not limited to the passage of time; everything is all here and now for him. He created us to live in eternity with him, forever, not subject to age, sickness, or death.

But in Adam and Eve we all sinned and became alienated from God and his life. We were headed for an eternity of misery and disconnection. In his mercy, God removed us from the Garden and put us into the world of time. Redemptive time began then. But it will not last forever. It will end when God redeems all things to himself, and once again all will be in eternity with him, as it was in the Beginning. As Jesus said, "I am the Alpha and the Omega, the Beginning and the End. To him who is thirsty I will give to drink without cost from the spring of the water of life" (Revelation 21:6).

Yet time is not a punishment for us. God did not take us out of eternity because he was mad at us. He was preserving us. He knew that we would be miserable in an eternity of brokenness. He knew we needed space to be repaired, healed, forgiven, and matured. He created time to be that space. It's a little like a hospital quarantining an operating room for a surgery, keeping it protected and safe, so that healing can occur through the doctor's skilled hands. As the surgeon, God redeems our lives and hearts over a process of time so that one day, when the work is finished, we will reenter eternity with him. This *redemptive time* provides the context for this process. It is our safety zone.

Your group can use this redemptive time in powerful ways. Over time, the necessary ingredients of grace and truth work healing on each person. Redemptive time can, of course, occur in intimate settings outside the group, such as prayer times, healthy conversations, and good connections between people. But make sure your group perceives the specific purpose and role of its time together. Let it take a timeless (eternal) flavor. As facilitator, you commit time and energy to be available, no matter how unready you feel. It is only reasonable to protect your group's time and experiences.

This may require you to gently guide things out of daily chitchat after a few minutes. Or you may have to help people move deeper than their everyday struggles to underlying themes and motivations. Don't worry about being someone's counselor. Rather, think about how few minutes a week most people get to be who they really are—with their hopes, injuries, and feelings—with other supportive people, and God, in the room. To be a facilitator of redemptive time is to provide something rare.

Group Goals Require Time for People to Grow and Develop

A group is, at heart, about life changes. Very few life changes occur instantly within a group setting. Most people join a group for things that will take time, such as:

- A better relationship with God and others
- Developing a skill
- Healing a wound from the past
- Self-control in a behavior that has the best of them
- Competence in a specific area, such as parenting, dating, or marriage
- Understanding themselves or others better

All of these, and any other topics you handle in your group, will require time. If people could gain such benefits instantly, chances are they wouldn't need to join a group to get them. But a group uses the process of time for its own gains and goals.

Would that things *could* be instant. We are an impatient species, and we are attracted to advertisements that promise weight loss or successful relationships or careers—right now. Understanding why change and growth in your group take time will help you and the members make use of the time, rather than fight it. Time always wins when we argue with it.

Change and Growth Are about Experience, Not Just Knowledge

True, deep, long-lasting changes occur through experiences with God and others that transform us from the inside out. Experiences cannot be shortchanged. Each requires time.

I remember talking to a man with a history of relational train wrecks. He could not find the "right" woman to date. He told me, "Okay, I have been reading you guys' books, and I get it. So what's next?"

I said, "Have you done what the books said?" He had not. He had just understood the principles, as he was a bright man.

I told him, "What you want is impossible until you get into a growth context to live out this material." He didn't like the idea and wanted to "get on with" his life. But he got into a good growth group. There he began finding out how afraid he was of relationship and how he tried to control others' perceptions of him. These realizations came through *experience*. He could have read a lot more books, but not been affected as profoundly as when he was face-to-face with people who were willing to love him enough to tell him the truth.

The Bible says it this way:

> Do not merely listen to the word, and so deceive yourselves. Do what it says. Anyone who listens to the word but does not do what it says is like a man who looks at his face in a mirror and, after looking at himself, goes away and immediately forgets what he looks like. But the man who looks intently into the perfect law that gives freedom, and continues to do this, not forgetting what he has heard, but doing it— he will be blessed in what he does (James 1:22–25).

Doing is experiencing. God created principles of growth and change that bless us when we experience them, not when we understand them. It is very different from learning or memorizing. Experience always takes more time than putting information into our heads, though that is important also. How comfortable would you be in a commercial plane if the pilot said, "Relax! I've only flown a time or two, but I aced the written test"? Good groups mean good growth experiences that occur over time. Make sure you allow time in your group for people to truly experience the information they are learning.

It Takes Time for People to Reveal Who They Really Are

The extent to which group members grow and change depends on how truly they get to know each other. Everyone starts off in a group with their best foot forward, and who can blame them? Most of the time you don't really know the members, so you put less-than-perfect parts of yourself on hold until you see how safe the group is. This process of gradually revealing hurts, weaknesses, sins, and failings requires time, and it is a good thing.

This is so important because the parts of ourselves that need the most help and healing are usually the parts we protect the most. Either these parts are inaccessible to us, or we are afraid of being shamed, put down, or hurt through exposure. We don't really come to a group for the strong, healthy, okay parts. So make sure your group provides time for people to gradually warm up, feel safe, and open up.

It Takes Time to Grow via Failure

Your group members want specific improvements and can only grow by taking risks, experiencing failure safely, learning from it, and trying again. There are no shortcuts. Failure is our master teacher, and those who do not know this teacher well tend to be short-termers in the growth process. It takes time to practice living out ways of being that frighten or elude us: "But solid food is for the mature, who because of practice have their senses trained to discern good and evil" (Hebrews 5:14 NASB). Practice brings failure, which brings relearning, which brings growth.

In a couples growth group, we were studying communication and "hearing" each other. We all thought we were pretty proficient in understanding our spouses until we went through a certain exercise. We couldn't make a discussion point till we had rephrased our spouse's point to his or her satisfaction. In other words, you don't move on until the spouse feels understood.

It was funny how bogged down our group got. It took a lot of time for us to find out that what we thought our spouses were saying was pretty far from what they were saying. It was like, "Honey, I think you are saying that you are bugged because I'm at work so much." "No, I'm not saying that at all. I'm saying that when you are home, you're not really here." "Oh! Let me try it again."

There was lots of failure. It took so much time. Yet it was really helpful to us. In your own group, create time and space for failure, and make it your friend.

Group Time Has Seasons

You may wonder sometimes why someone in your group feels stuck, why members don't seem to be on the same page, or why the group isn't coming together. One reason is that people and groups have their own seasons. As Solomon wrote, "There is a time for everything, and a season for every activity under heaven: a time to be born and a time to die, a time to plant and a time to uproot, a time to kill and a time to heal, a time to tear down and a time to build" (Ecclesiastes 3:1–3).

A group member who seems engaged in the group yet doesn't seem to "get it" may simply be in a winter of the soul. Bleak discouragement, perhaps over a relational conflict or career frustration, may drive her to desire a group. She may come to the group more in touch with her problems than with God's hope. You can encourage her to see this seemingly unfruitful time as a time of clearing out obstacles to make way for new growth.

Group time can enter a season of spring when members allow themselves to be known, both good and bad parts, and begin to connect. This universality of shared experience gives them new hope that if they invest in God and others, they will reap later.

Just as summer brings a great deal of growth, your group will see life changes through getting closer and experiencing grace, truth, forgiveness, and correction. During this time of gratification, some people may be tempted to stop sowing. Be aware of this tendency, and encourage members to stick with the process for the deeper fruit ahead.

The fall harvest comes as parents see their children mature and become more responsible, people dealing with bad habits experience freedom, and people working on relationships find doors unlocked inside themselves and loved ones. People see that allowing time for group processes really does work. This may also be a good time for the group to change topics, multiply into new groups, or deepen group ties.

The seasonal metaphor reminds us that groups operate over time—weeks, months, years, and sometimes decades. But remember that time alone does not heal or fix people. Rather, time is the vehicle through which the appropriate grace and truth do their spiritual growth work within group members' hearts.

Chapter 4

Benefits of Groups That Grow

When I (John) was in college, I was involved in Christian and nonreligious small groups on campus. I enjoyed getting together, and I gained much from these groups. But I will never forget the night that for me instantly transformed a Christian college group to a Group.

The group was an informal combination of Bible study, discussion, and life sharing. I liked all the things I was learning, I liked the people, and it was interesting. I felt that God was using it to help me grow. Dan, the facilitator, was a warm, personable student a couple of years older than the rest of us. I was drawn by his attitude and maturity. One night, however, he started the group by saying, "Hey, I am really struggling with lust and sexual temptation, and I need to let you guys know what is going on so you can help me and pray for me." As he talked about the struggle, a chain reaction occurred; the rest of us started chiming in about how tough the sexual purity battle was for us, too.

This may be normal for your group, but for me it was world shattering. It was my first experience of sane, healthy, open discussion with other guys about sex. Until then any conversation I'd had about sex had been limited to two categories: not so edifying, or quick, embarrassed agreement that we should avoid sexual sin. But that night Dan helped us open up our lives, hearts, and emotions. I came away pretty shaken up inside, but in a good way. I felt connected to the other guys in a way I had never experienced before. It was as if deeper parts of me had a place to go, where we were all the same.

What had become a Group didn't talk about sex every week, but the people and what happened there became more important to me. Something changed within me. Though I still got the same things I'd originally come to the group for—spiritual growth, learning, friendship—I began receiving another spiritual benefit I hadn't signed up for. That surprising benefit was the possibility of being connected, heart and soul, to God and others without having to edit, pretend, or hold back.

My point is that *small groups provide benefits beyond the scope of their context, topic, or materials.* While what people learn is very important, the group experience itself changes members' hearts in subtle ways. The beneficial connections created through the small group experience produce other fundamental benefits that have to do with what the Bible calls *sanctification,* being set apart and cleansed for God's service. These benefits are honesty, integration of character, and normalizing struggle. Thus small groups help heal, grow, mature, and repair people so they are fit and ready to be used by and for God. Small groups are that important.

The Bible teaches that all of life has consequences: "Do not be deceived: God cannot be mocked. A man reaps what he sows" (Galatians 6:7). We often see only the warning part of this passage, but the reality is that squarely facing real life and its consequences can be good and positive, not just painful and negative. Loving, responsible, and honest sowing can produce a good harvest for us. The rewarding consequences of being in a growing small group make it worth all the time we spend sowing our lives in them.

Connectedness

People in a growing group soon notice what I experienced in my college group: *You are not alone; you belong somewhere.* We neither survive nor thrive in a vacuum, isolated from others. God the Creator designed us to live life not only with him, but also with each other. True life lies in relationship: "It is not good that the man should be alone" (Genesis 2:18 KJV). Research has illustrated what the Bible teaches about the necessity of connectedness. People who are deeply attached to others tend to live longer, better, and more healthily.

At the same time, we tend to isolate and pull away into ourselves, via workaholism, self-sufficiency, and busyness or because we fear closeness. For some people, the easiest route in life is away from connectedness and toward aloneness. It means fewer problems and less risk. If you're all you have, at least you can trust yourself.

Given this tendency, we do not always gravitate toward the connectedness we need. This is where groups come in. Groups provide a framework for relationship and connectedness. This connectedness produces specific benefits.

Groups Create Three Important Connections

Connections within the group occur as the group takes on a "family" role. Rather than being a mini-seminar, with all attendees focused on learning from a speaker (a recipe for group disaster), people get to know each other in personal ways. They open up about their lives, losses, and difficulties. They give and receive with each other. Between group meetings you find yourself wondering how Jill is doing with her dating situation, or you read a Bible passage and think that it might encourage Trent in his parenting.

Connections outside the group grow as connectedness becomes a way of life. The group requires it, and then that way becomes translated into all of life. Experiencing relationship in a group gives members a model to relate to their spouses, dates, families, kids, friends, and coworkers. They become more relationally oriented. Many times I have heard a husband of a group member tell me, "I am getting so much out of whatever she is doing in her group." Usually that means that the safety and honesty that the member is receiving in the group is becoming part of the marriage outside the group.

Closer connections with God develop as people connect in the group. Our vertical disconnection often has to do with our horizontal disconnection. Whatever keeps us from loving others can prevent us from loving God: "For anyone who does not love his brother, whom he has seen, cannot love God, whom he has not seen" (1 John 4:20). However, as group members become more able to trust, depend on, and open up to each other, they find that God seems more real, personal, and accessible.

Groups Provide Benefits

The connectedness developed through groups provides specific benefits to group members.

Our problems seem less overwhelming. When we are alone, life situations seem massive and unfixable. As we have said earlier, if you could have fixed things without a group, you probably would have by now. But when you are connected to people who are with and for you, you receive encouragement, perspective, and resources you cannot manufacture on your own. I have seen many group members more able to face reality simply because they brought the group into it. Whether or not other members gave advice or wisdom, the ones who shared knew they were not alone anymore. That knowledge gave more ability to face and deal with the problem.

We see need and dependency as strengths the more we understand the benefits of being connected. Dependent, needy emotions are God's gifts when they drive us to each other.

This is also a special benefit for those with codependent tendencies. Codependents—technically, people who are dependent on dependent people—often have great difficulty allowing themselves to need others. They are much more able to connect as givers and providers rather than as receivers. Group connectedness helps them see this as a problem; they confront this imbalance as something that keeps people away from them.

From this, the codependents learn to work through their fears or guilt about having needs, and they experience receiving love and support.

We experience all of ourselves in the warmth and safety of a good group. This context helps people know themselves better. They discover feelings and abilities they never knew existed, because they were never in a safe enough place for those things to emerge. I remember a woman who had never grieved over her daughter's tragic death. Her background had trained her to be positive and strong, to get over something impossible for most of us to grasp. However, in a safe group she rediscovered the deep love and loss she felt about her daughter. With their support, she truly said good-bye to her daughter and gradually moved on.

We resolve self-judgment. Alienated from ourselves and others, we feel self-critical, judging, or inadequate. Isolated people often experience themselves as "bad" people. There is not enough grace and love inside them to deal with their failures and imperfections. A group setting is a delivery system for that grace to enter their heads and hearts and, while not putting them into denial about their issues, gives them the ability to look at, accept, and work on the issues from a loved position rather than a judged position. When we are all alone with who we really are, we often experience the Law in its fury: it truly "brings wrath" (Romans 4:15). Many times I have seen a person bring some part of himself out of disconnection and alienation into the group—and then get out of the prison of self-hatred into acceptance.

Honesty

When we contemplate telling the truth to someone, many of us often end up avoiding it. We just anticipate too much tension and conflict. Yet, when we become settled into good group connections, we can receive the courage to acknowledge reality, tell the truth, and welcome it from others.

In growing groups, members learn the value of telling the truth to each other and to themselves. Many people are afraid of honesty because of their life experiences. They have learned that honesty makes others angry, that people might withhold love from them, that it harms others, or that they themselves have been wounded by the truth. So they do all they can to avoid the negativity and risk of honesty. Of course, then they fall into the imbalance of never being able to correct and solve life problems.

By contrast, in growing groups, members experience how healing and freeing the truth can be when it is administered in a "no condemnation" environment. They find that people don't fall apart and have tantrums when confronted. Instead, conflicts are resolved and relationships get better. They find that their perspective has something to offer someone else, and their viewpoint is helpful and valuable. And probably most important, they experience that they can receive the truth about themselves and still feel love and grace. So they are free to accept loving feedback and correction and make needed changes that create an even better life for themselves.

Valuing honesty also makes members more aware of deception, manipulation, and control in their lives outside the group. The truthfulness born and nurtured in the group gives them a sort of "lie radar" they didn't have before. They begin to require honesty in life and to deal with its absence.

Integration of Character

Groups also foster integration in the character of their members. This technical-sounding term explains an important biblical concept. Integration is *the state of accepting, experiencing, and dealing with all parts of ourselves, good and bad.* That is, an integrated person lives in self-aware reality rather than just experiencing parts of that reality. The Bible teaches that the opposite of integration—what James called being "double-minded" (1:8) or, as the Greek indicates, "two-spirited"—causes instability in our lives.

Lack of integration can take many forms.

- Perfectionist tendencies make it difficult for people to accept who they really are and to grow from there.
- Idealism and naïveté keep people from seeing negatives about themselves or others; therefore, those realities blindside them.
- Shame and guilt encourage hiding and pretending.

- Black-and-white thinking keeps people from resolving life issues, as they can't see a situation's gray area or middle ground.
- Denial makes people unable to see or be aware of some important reality.
- A secret life or behavior controls people.
- Fragmentation makes people seem all over the place, unable to focus on anything because of the chaos within.

In all of the above scenarios, the people suffer from some inability to be all they are; their "two spirits" keep their lives divided and not working as God intended. Lack of integration tears up relationships, careers, and hope.

Groups are a powerful force to develop integration, because the group setting becomes a safe structure for people to become aware of feared or lost parts of themselves, often because the group is aware of them. The group lets the person know there is no condemnation. Just as a good family helps a child become aware of and address her strengths and weaknesses, the group encourages all parts of its members to come out.

The result is that members learn to accept themselves, stop hiding and pretending, and live in the reality of who they truly are. They experience growth and change in their problem areas. Furthermore, the integrated member also develops a better life in the "real world." He is more of himself in love, family, and friendships. He has less conflict, nothing to hide.

When Joe, a guy I know, started in a growth group, he was tightly wound. He was pleasant, but very concerned about looking and acting appropriate so as not to upset anyone. He deferred to everyone. Of course, while being nice was positive, he also had trouble in his dating life, because the women would say he wasn't "real." For the same reason, bosses at work didn't promote him.

The group loved and accepted Joe. They also confronted the nice guy part, saying, "Joe, sometimes we think you agree with everything less than you say you do." They encouraged his more honest self to come out and be integrated with the rest of him.

At first Joe thought the group didn't appreciate his attempts to please them. Actually, he was right; they didn't. But he could tell they loved him and saw more in him than he did. Gradually, a more emotional and sometimes rebellious self began to emerge. He found himself having new opinions and feelings.

Joe even went through a mini-adolescent rebellion, wearing counter-culture clothes and hairstyles. The group stayed with him and, while helping him not do anything destructive, loved him as he was. Slowly, Joe integrated his more confrontational and opinionated parts into his love and caring, and he settled down as a maturing adult. His dating life and career also improved.

The point is this: We all need a place to accept, experience, and integrate all parts of ourselves in an atmosphere of love and safety. Help your group to be that place.

Normalizing Struggle

Henry and I have been presenting a Monday night seminar for many years in Southern California. One night I spoke on dealing with pain and struggle. I started off with a question for the audience: "Why in the world would anyone want a talk on pain? It's such a downer." A guy in the back yelled out, "'Cause it's there anyway!"

I had to agree. Issues such as failure, conflict, pain, and struggle, though negative in nature, are "there." They exist, whether we want them to or not. Much of our life depends on how we address and handle these issues. The Bible teaches that since the Fall, we exist in a world of pain. Speaking of humankind, Solomon says, "All his days his work is pain and grief; even at night his mind does not rest" (Ecclesiastes 2:23).

This is the situation we live in now. It will not always be that way. At the end of time, pain will be no more: "There will be no more death or mourning or crying or pain, for the old order of things has passed away" (Revelation 21:4). Until then, we experience all sorts of negativity, in ourselves, in others, and in the world.

We tend to avoid pain. We try not to focus on it and pretend it isn't there, minimize its effect on us, blame it on others, anesthetize it, and so on. But the best thing we can do is learn to deal with it well. One great benefit of groups is helping people to *normalize,* or adjust and adapt to and deal with, pain and struggle. While we may not enjoy failure and conflict, we surely benefit when we know what to do about them.

An underlying assumption of any good group is that all members are expected to make mistakes and to bring those mistakes before the group. When they engage in this process, they find that they don't struggle alone; there is a universality of suffering among the members. They realize that others do not reject them, but rather draw closer to them. They give up their protests and accept mistakes, pain, and failure as a part of life and growth. They end their unrealistic expectations of others and accept others as they also have been accepted. They become less rigid and anxious, and more flexible, because unexpected problems don't get them off balance. They learn mature traits such as patience, perseverance, forgiveness, and self-control. Sound like a good return on your investment? Groups can create an atmosphere in which dealing well with pain and struggle provides many good things within us.

The converse is also true. If a group attempts to avoid these matters, the results can be quite dramatic. Personal change will occur on the surface, not deep inside, and it will not be long lasting. People become externally oriented, rather than internally oriented. They remain impatient, looking for quick results now, rather than diligently waiting for results over time. They are more focused on others' treatment of them (third person) rather than focused on the relationships that really matter in the group (first and second person). Basically, their lives don't improve in whatever arenas they are coming to the group to address, because they have no tools or encouragement to deal with life's negatives.

Groups involve a commitment and investment of each member's life, energy, and heart. Yet, over time, this sort of investment has great rewards and returns. Keep the fruits of connectedness, honesty, integration, and pain normalization as key benefits of your group's activities and processes.

PART 2

WHAT HAPPENS
IN A GOOD GROUP

Introduction

In this section we present the specific tasks that effective groups perform to produce the best growth. Understanding these tasks will help you as the leader to choose the activities and attitudes that promote the most growth during the group time. This is a practical section. We intend to give you a mental picture of what happens in a good group, so you can recognize it in your own group. Some tasks have similar functions but more than one intent or result. For example, a good group experience validates both the person who needs strengthening and the person who needs healing. As we hope you will find, however, the tasks all work together in an integrated fashion as the group grows up its members.

Chapter 5

A Second Family

An important aspect of any growth-producing group is that it provides a context for members to reexperience whatever they missed in life the first time around. The second time they may gain and develop that missing part. This may be from the ground up, as in childhood, or it may be some lesson or ability never mastered in adulthood. But the group operates as a place to start all over again in fundamental areas and, this time, learn and experience things in the right way.

Second Chance Requires Humility

Groups are like a second family for people. Whatever needs their original families or environments did not provide, or whatever they provided that the person did not need, the group restores and repairs. It is a second chance. Like little children, members should come with immaturities and needs, and the group helps them move to the next stage.

Groups of people working like that repairing family are a large part of God's process of maturing us: "God sets the lonely in families" (Psalm 68:6).

The relearning aspect of groups requires that members take on the humility of a child. A toddler is aware that he needs love, protection, and acceptance from his parents. He naturally looks to them when he wants something from them. In the same way, the group creates an environment such that everyone must gain what is needed by reaching out to others.

Most people don't come by this childlike stance easily. They may think they have no issues or may minimize the ones they admit. They may be discouraged or skeptical that group can truly help them. They may be set in their patterns. This is why you may need to spend time developing the expectation that group requires members to become open to learning new life patterns. Help them to accept the possibility that something transforming can happen in the meeting.

Group is much more than connecting and being known, though both make up the foundation of a group. Much of the real work involves internalizing experiences that help a person gain tools and abilities for handling life. Connection and safety create an environment in which people can take the risks they need to grow and repair. The best groups focus on both emotional connections and members' current tasks and issues.

Some people need to learn to receive grace and love instead of pushing it away or diverting it back to the giver. Others need to be honest about how defensive they get when they are confronted. Some need to learn that sadness is an emotion they must embrace. Still others must learn how to "be angry . . . and sin not" (Ephesians 4:26 KJV), that is, to make anger a relational experience and know how to appropriately confess and use it.

For example, a woman may come in with no ability to be clear, defined, and honest about what she will and will not put up with. Perhaps she came from a family in which she was the peacekeeper and kept everyone happy. She may have suffered from her inability, becoming lost in controlling relationships and enabling people. Perhaps her church background supported her inability to take responsibility for her own life.

The "second family" can be a safe place for this woman to gain what she never received from her family or church. Group members can encourage her to be honest. They can provide materials, books, and biblical principles on why truthfulness is good. They can assure her that her truth, even her anger, will be accepted and welcome as an authentic part of her. They can help her work through her fears and anxieties about being a bad or unloving person if she says no or confronts people. They can role-play honesty scenarios with her. They can confront her when she is silent, passive, or indirect. They can represent people she fears being honest with, such as aggressive types, introverts, or folks who appear successful. Basically, the group provides all the elements she still needs to learn *by experience*. Thus she gains the growth, healing, and competency that life requires of her.

The Better Way: Worth the Effort

For some people this description of group characteristics may be new and unfamiliar terrain. As a facilitator you may be thinking, *I just wanted to help people support each other; this sounds like too big a deal.* We don't want anyone to feel intimidated by the prospect of doing groups. Always remember that as a group leader you are a *facilitator* of growth. Much of the responsibility for growth rests with the members and what they do with the meeting.

At the same time, do realize that groups really are about the stuff of life and growth. Their power and potential cannot be overestimated. Groups provide a unique opportunity for many ingredients of growth and healing to intermingle. For some people, the group context can be the best, most profound, and most growth-producing set of experiences they have ever had or will have.

It is tempting to play it safe and decide only to study some material, with no personal interaction. You might choose to avoid talking about struggle and keep things light and positive. In fact, in the proper context some good can come from groups like these.

For the best and most life-changing results, however, we believe it is better to involve people's whole hearts, souls, and minds. Help them talk face-to-face with each other about each other. Give them the experiences they never had safety or grace to have. Help them meet God in a deeper and more meaningful way. Our experience is that most people who take the time, energy, commitment, and risk to formally join a group are motivated by real-life needs: to know God and others, heal a hurt, reach their potential or goals and dreams, repair a weakness, develop an ability, integrate a lost part of themselves, or get control over something. Don't be afraid of truly becoming the family they need so they can move on in life and accomplish what God has called them to be and do.

Chapter 6

Connection

Groups connect. That is, they bring people together on a personal and heart-based level. Connection is the basis of any good work in a group. For a few minutes every week or so, members receive the experience of being attached, loved, and in relationship with like-minded people. Connection, far more than the information dispensed, keeps people coming to group. When people feel attached, they become much more invested in the process, and their hearts become more open to God, growth, and each other. As Paul entreated his friends, "As a fair exchange—I speak as to my children—open wide your hearts also" (2 Corinthians 6:13). There are several ways that connection takes place.

Connection Elements in the Group

Each group takes on the responsibility of being a place where connection can be created and flourish. This includes elements such as safety, nonjudgmentalism, honesty, and a process orientation. The group talks about these elements and invites members to say whether they are experiencing sufficient amounts of these elements. For example, someone might say, "Does anyone have a concern about how safe the group is, so that you can open up with whatever is going on?" Someone else might respond, "I'd like to talk about things going on with me, but last week it seemed that when someone mentioned a failure in their life, everyone jumped all over her. That pretty much shut me down." A good group constantly makes sure that what is needed for connection is present.

Group Materials Build Connection

If the group is a study group with organized materials, such as on spiritual growth, marriage, or relationships, the members interact with the study in terms of their hearts and attachments to each other. For example, one person may say, "After we went over the section about being vulnerable in life, I realized I'm avoiding that here in the group."

Discussion Content Is Connection-Oriented

The content of a group is what people bring up to talk about. In connecting groups, the content can be personal, emotional, or struggle based. It is sometimes risky. It is more than principles and information, though that can be a part. Basically, people are opening up their hearts and lives to each other, and connections are being built.

In a good group you will notice that the discussion content is generally not what would be talked about in a conference, which is more learning and information, nor what would be in an informal gathering of friends, which is more catching up on the events of life. It has more to do with private, personal, and transcendent themes, which few people regularly bring out into the light of day. When the members leave the group meeting, they know they have connected in a way that the rest of life doesn't provide for them.

Group Members Expect to Discuss Their Relationships

Groups actively talk about their relationships within the group. It is normal to discuss opening up, trusting someone, and the particular relationships with one another. Sometimes there's a flow between a growth topic and the relationships, but the group never neglects the connections. Even when good groups are discussing a most interesting subject, they notice and address if someone is hurting and detached. When I (John) have led groups that had a lot of tension between people, I have often stopped the discussion and said, "There's something going on in between a couple of people here. Let's talk about it."

Conversely, a common sign of a group's getting out of balance is discussion weighted toward people who aren't in the room, such as troubles members are having with a spouse, child, friend, or date. While this is certainly important information, over time it does not create the life change that talking *to each other about our experience of each other* brings. Good groups spend significant time helping the members open up themselves to each other, giving validation, love, comfort, feedback, and confrontation.

Groups Monitor Their Relationships

Group members learn to be aware, on an ongoing basis, of how attached the group is. Connections can happen both gradually and every few seconds. The gradual aspect shows that only time, risk, and experience develop intimacy in a group. All things being equal, a group that has been working on connecting for a year will be further along in intimacy than one just starting out. Members observe whether or not, over time, they are becoming closer and more open to each other. The second aspect has to do with how people's emotions shift as they relate to each other, and this must be monitored, too. This is called *immediacy*, and it is an important part of a connection. For example, one person may say, "It seems like you withdrew when Alice was mentioning her dating life. Is there anything going on right now?" The group is aware of these changes in connections.

Chapter 7

Discipline and Structure

You will always see an element of discipline and structure in a good group. Though the group is based on a foundation of grace and acceptance, it also requires order and responsibility through clear expectations about members' attendance, involvement, and participation.

Discipline Protects the Group

Good groups use discipline and structure to protect the time, the process, and the members from disruption. They understand that safety only comes when things are somewhat predictable and when people know that out-of-control behavior, for example, will be confronted and addressed. This is not about being mean, harsh, or punitive. It is about helping the group function as it should.

I (John) remember one member who, when angry, would verbally attack other members. People were thinking of quitting group. After many attempts to help her with this, I finally told her that if she attacked people that severely one more time, I would ask her to leave. It happened, and I did, and she left. It was really painful for her and all of us, but in the end, the group did better, and she eventually created a growth context that was a better fit for her as well.

Group structure and discipline also help those who need internal limits and perhaps struggle with impulsiveness or disorganization. Internalizing group expectations helps the member form better self-control, restraint, and responsibility. Good groups will insist on certain rules of conduct as a requirement for membership. This isn't about a lack of grace or acceptance. Rather, it's about applying grace and acceptance as a framework for people's lives. They experience the combination of grace and discipline rather than experiencing them separately.

For example, in one group I led, a couple of people kept coming late. It was hard on the group, as the late person would enter the room just as someone was getting into a painful or embarrassing topic. The latecomer would try to be quiet, apologizing as she found her seat, but it was difficult. You didn't know whether to keep going, knowing the late person didn't know the situation; or to catch her up, which got people out of the experience and into their heads again; or to bring up the lateness, which again destroyed the moment.

The group very graciously discussed the difficulties of lateness with the offenders. One only had to hear it once, and she was so concerned about how her lateness affected others that she was never late again. Another, however, had a lot of excuses about kids, traffic, and work—all problems that the rest of the group also contended with. Though she said she understood the issue, she still thought events were beyond her control, and she continued coming late.

Finally I came up with a plan. We all agreed that when group started at the appointed time, we closed the door and got going. Any latecomer had to wait outside the meeting room while group went on. When the group reached a point that they could transition to some other topic or person without a lot of disruption, we would go out and get the late person. This minimized the distraction of the late person, and it helped her to experience what it was like to miss out on the connections in the group.

The approach worked. After a couple of times, the late person started getting there on time because she wanted to be involved. We all cheered her when she started showing up on time. In fact, she reported to us that this discipline was helping her be more structured and focused in her outside life, where it was also a problem.

When I applied the "time out" structure to another group with a similar problem, the result was different. For a long time, the chronically late member missed the beginning of every session. The group was vulnerable, let her know they missed her, let her know how it affected them, and continued caring. But she always had a different excuse.

I used to think this application of group discipline failed. But as I thought about it, I realized that, though it failed with this person, it succeeded in protecting the group. So in that sense, it did its job.

How to Discipline with Love

A good group will keep love, connection, and growth as first priorities. The following guidelines will help you use the discipline and structure of meetings to minimize chaos, disruptions, and acting out so members experience good things.

See the love in discipline. Help people take the sting out of discipline and show them that it involves love. Ask about times they experienced discipline as hurtful or condemning. Talk about the benefits of gently bringing structure to each other's lives.

See the need. Group members can discuss the times when their lack of structure hurt themselves or someone else. For example, one might say, "I wish I had had someone around me when I was in my financial crisis, to help me see that the easy choices weren't the best choices."

Learn a language of discipline. Good groups know how to talk about discipline and structure to each other so that the connections are kept alive. For example, the leader may say, "Okay, Randy, I'm not picking on you, but everybody did their lesson this week except you. This is the fourth time it's happened. I think people may be feeling disconnected from you, like you're not really invested in the group. What if someone calls you during the week to see how the lesson is going?"

Learn how much structure the group needs. Some groups need very little, as the people may have a great deal of internal structure. Other groups, whose members have a hard time being organized or dependable, may require more structure.

Above all, good groups see discipline and structure as important ways to keep members together through growth: "He who ignores discipline despises himself, but whoever heeds correction gains understanding" (Proverbs 15:32).

Chapter 8

Prayer

Prayer can be one of the small group's most powerful tools for growth. God designed prayer as a way for people to connect with him for all the blessings of life. When we are present in groups in his name, Jesus is there, too: "For where two or three come together in my name, there am I with them" (Matthew 18:20).

Coming together for prayer in small groups connects people with God and each other. Corporate prayer brings people together in their faith and love for God and in their dependence on him and each other. It draws us close, vertically and horizontally.

Decide Prayer's Place in Your Group

There is a range of involvement with prayer, depending on your group. Some groups allocate a dedicated time for prayer; some open or close with prayer; some allow spontaneous prayer. There are also times when group or corporate prayer might not be appropriate. This could possibly be the case with a seeker-oriented group that is reaching out to nonbelievers.

Discuss Prayer's Involvement with the Members

Whatever you have decided about the place of prayer, make sure everyone knows and is on board with it. Often, people who are comfortable with group prayer will be insensitive to the difficulty of those with little experience. You might say, "We believe that God comes closer to us, and we to him, when we pray for people's concerns in a group. If you are uncomfortable, let's talk about it. Maybe it could be an area you want to develop, or if not, maybe you can just be present and connected silently."

Give Freedom

Prayer comes best from the heart. Help people feel open and vulnerable to God in the same way they try to be in group. Let them be free to say what they need to say to the Lord.

Pray about Group Issues

Help people get beyond the idea that God is concerned only about catastrophes and health issues. Teach them to pray for each other's brokenness, relationships, stuck places, connections, answers, and growth steps. For example, you might pray, "God, please help Cynthia keep her boundaries this week with her kids."

Guide People to Expect God's Response and Healing

It's exciting when small group members pray in specific terms, especially regarding group concerns, and then see God bring fruit out of their requests. Faith is strengthened, and people feel closer to each other. I remember our group praying for God to bring about a breakthrough for a man who couldn't figure out what was keeping him from taking emotional risks. Soon afterward, he became aware of a strong fear that people would leave him, and the group helped him resolve it over time, as then he and they knew in what direction to go.

Introduce Group Prayer for Other Concerns

Have the group pray for important matters beyond the group. For example, pray corporately for your church, community, country, and leadership.

Have Spirit-led Prayer

Lead the group in seeking God without an agenda and instead remaining sensitive to him and his leading. Help your group to connect with God and each other in prayer. When we pray, God answers in many unexpected ways: "Call to me and I will answer you and tell you great and unsearchable things you do not know" (Jeremiah 33:3).

Chapter 9

Accountability

Today *accountability* is one of the most misunderstood terms in both spiritual growth thinking and small group thinking. It actually means *to be answerable*. In other words, members are answerable, or give an accounting of themselves, to each other. They bring their struggles and failures to the group, are honest about them, own them, and let the group respond to them in growth-producing ways.

However, for some groups, accountability is basically a reporting function. The person shows up and reports a failure to the group; the group forgives him and then says to try not to do it again. While all this is important, it is not enough for growth, and this misunderstanding misses the mark of what accountability is and does. Worse, some weaker groups use accountability to punish the person. They operate with shame and guilt. They make confession feel embarrassing, because they think the negative experience will deter or shame the person into gaining self-control over a problem. Most of the time, however, this simply helps the person hide better or find an excuse to quit the group. While reducing accountability to a reporting function is better than making it a shameful experience, it still misses the mark of healthy accountability.

True Accountability

In good groups, accountability involves the *whole person*. That is, the members bring all of themselves to the group: behavior, attitudes, insides, and externals. Growth happens when we show up to group in heart, mind, soul, and strength. For example, a man may be concerned about sexual temptation and Internet porn. He brings the issue to the group and makes himself answerable to the group for this. At each meeting the man lets the group in on the week's successes and failures. But accountability doesn't stop there in a good group. The member also reveals to the group what drives the temptation: internal lacks or inabilities, stresses, and circumstantial triggers to acting out.

The group is then involved in helping the struggling member not just with acts, but with his entire life. Their approach to him works the same way. They hear his confession of victories or defeats, and that is helpful. If we know that what we do will be revealed to those who love us, it helps us have more control than if we live in darkness. But at the same time, the group members also hold the man accountable *for being in the process of growth and repair.* They ask him about his loneliness and isolation, impulsiveness, or fears of conflict. In other words, they ask about whatever is causing or driving the problem. They have him answer to them about what he is doing about these underlying issues. They want to know if he is bringing those parts of himself to them for repair and healing as much as he is bringing the "fruit" of all that, which is the act itself. One of the most important aspects is that they hold him accountable to his other program.

Encouraging Individual Accountability

Then there is the aspect of individual accountability in contrast with group accountability. That is, all members will have a certain stance on their answerability to others, and good groups pay attention to this individual accountability. For example, some people with a high degree of ownership and responsibility will readily bring problems and failures to the group, because they understand that this is the path to healing. They desire the benefits of bringing their struggles and issues to the group. They feel no need to escape the group's scrutiny, nor to be defensive and seen as having it "together." The group can use the following suggestions to help members less ready to be individually accountable.

Lovingly confront a low sense of accountability. Ask why this member isn't talking about real issues or evident problems. Group members can tell the person that they want her to take initiative to talk about what's going on rather than them having to hunt down and drag it out. Sometimes the group will discover that the person still carries great wounds from being judged and condemned elsewhere in life. For her, accountability is torture. The group helps heal that in her so she experiences the acceptance that goes along with true accountability. In others, the group will find a lifelong pattern of irresponsibility, immaturity, or blame. This person will find that the group, while loving, will also instruct him on accountability's importance, their experiences with it, and hopefully, how much they want to be involved in that better way with the person.

Make grace-filled accountability a group norm. In every scenario, the healthy group intends to make accountability loving, grace-filled, expected, and participated in by every member. Individuals learn that being monitored does not mean having a parent looking over their shoulder. Rather, it means answering to others so they can be healed at deep levels. That's how accountability performs its growth tasks.

Discuss people's impressions of accountability. Do they see accountability as "reporting to Dad"? Does it provoke anxiety? Does it make them dread coming to group? Help them sort out old preconceptions.

Give them the big picture of accountability. Help them move beyond the idea that accountability merely means confessing to another person. Help them see it as more about helping people to bring growth and struggle issues to the relationship so that the process of healing can happen. A leader might say, "We don't want to be accountable to each other just to keep each other in line. We want to be accountable to each other so we can look at where we are broken and unable."

Help them experience true accountability. When someone wants to avoid working on an issue and simply confesses it, say, "Tom, you've brought up your temper several times to the group, and yet it doesn't seem to be getting better. What if we hold you accountable to talking about how helpless and sad you feel when you're under stress?"

Show how it works in the group. When people experience the blessings of accountability, they are more likely to get on board. For example, "Sarah, the next time I negate your opinion or idea, I want you to say something about it right then, because I'm not aware of it. And I want anyone else in the group to do the same thing."

Chapter 10

Forgiveness

Healthy groups powerfully administer grace and forgiveness, the foundation from which all growth and healing stems. Good groups are based on, and are full of, grace and forgiveness. There really can be no lasting life change without these ingredients.

Grace speaks to our weakness and inability, forgiveness to our many failures. Weakness, inability, and failure are the main reasons we need group, so that we may be strengthened in many areas of life. Without grace and forgiveness, the truth cannot come out. This could be the truth members need to admit to themselves, the truth they need to confess to others, the truth they need to receive from others, or the truth they need to confront others with. Without a basis of grace and forgiveness, truth becomes too painful, harsh, and condemning. That is why the Bible teaches us to "be kind and compassionate to one another, forgiving each other, just as in Christ God forgave you" (Ephesians 4:32). Make grace and forgiveness evident in every meeting. As we receive these gifts, so should we administer them to one another.

Hallmarks Evident in Every Meeting

As we discussed in chapter 3, grace is an essential ingredient of growth. The best definition of *grace* is *unmerited favor*, that God is "for" us and we cannot earn that status. This stance is borne out in the group process. You will notice that the members are on one another's side. This does not mean that they agree on everything or never confront; rather, they fundamentally desire the best for each other. A group based on grace stays "for" its members, no matter what is said or done.

The group is a source of grace to its members. Grace is freely given to all, in the same way it was given to us by God. The group never puts someone in grace or out of grace because of how they are doing in the process. Grace is stable and consistent and flows to all because that is how God designed it.

In addition, forgiveness, the cancellation of a debt, is seen as a norm and is expected in the group. Grace gives people the safety and courage to expose their weaknesses and frailties; forgiveness releases them from their debt to the law and frees them to start afresh. People come into the group burdened with failures, sins, and guilt. The group forgives, thus freeing and restoring its members. There is no demand for revenge or punishment in a healthy group, only the desire for the person to experience forgiveness and make the changes necessary to move on.

Grace and forgiveness operate when the members lovingly show equal interest in someone's failures as in their victories; when compassion is waiting for the person who finally opens up about a shameful weakness; when someone says, "Thanks for opening up about your struggle. I know that was not easy." This experience of grace is often not readily found in other areas of our lives.

The group understands that there is no division within itself of people who are okay and those who aren't okay. Every member is a broken person who needs repair and restoration but cannot fix himself. Often the members who have been the most broken have also received the most grace and forgiveness; therefore they will have the most to offer. Groups or group members new to the experience—or not very open about failure and inability—tend to be shallow in grace and have less to offer.

Administering Grace and Forgiveness

Furthermore, growing groups *expect and invite the very things that require grace and forgiveness.* That is, the group is aware that its members have needs, inabilities, and failures that require grace to heal, grow, and change. The group doesn't focus on the positive aspects of life at the expense of those realities. The following six tips will help your grace-based group seek out and encourage people to expose and confess aspects of their lives that deeply need love and forgiveness.

Dig deeper. Members can dig a little deeper into someone's story or sharing, sensing who is trying to avoid pain. They want to know the person more deeply, *for it is at that level that people most need, and can use, grace and forgiveness.*

Push a bit. Good groups sometimes push a person to see or own that what he does is hurtful, so he can receive the healing he needs. The member who experiences little vulnerability is seen as aberrant rather than the norm. Members confront his distance, denial, or self-sufficiency so he can come to terms with his need for grace that the group then freely offers.

Talk about the meanings of grace and forgiveness. Help members understand that these are the foundation of the group and their own growth.

Create the right environment. Group members might say to each other, "How can I help make it okay for you to feel enough grace to open up?" The other may say, "I need reassurance (or eye contact or warmth or silence)."

Experience grace and forgiveness. When someone opens up about a failure or loss, help people be present with that person: "Tell us more. We are on your side."

Make failure an expected event. When someone avoids bringing up problems, say, "It's hard to feel close to you right now because I'm so aware of my own faults that I bring up here, and you don't present any."

Chapter 11

Support and Strengthening

Support and strengthening indicate that a group is doing the right things. When members become weak or discouraged, groups can help them become stronger and better able to handle life. Groups take our weakness and transform it into strength. People who can admit their weakness can also receive the strength the group offers, while those who must stay strong miss this blessing: "For when I am weak, then I am strong" (2 Corinthians 12:10).

As people begin to open up in group—whether about faith, relationship struggle, or a personal battle—they bring up things they simply don't have the strength or courage to tackle, handle, or even face. These are the substance of group work, as they require group intervention and strengthening.

Attending

Groups do many things that assist and support. One thing they do is *attend*. Members listen with their entire being, putting their own experiences on the back burner to enter another's world. Truly listening to someone dealing with weakness helps that person feel that the issue is not as unmanageable as he feared. It diminishes his sense of isolation. Members in a group *look* at the person talking; they are emotionally *there* with him.

Validation

Groups also strengthen members through validation, confirming a person's emotional reality. People who struggle need to know that others understand how bad it really is and how bad they feel inside. When the group says, "We believe you; this is scary and bad for you," you might think it would make the person feel even worse, but it actually builds her up. When a person's feelings are dismissed, she is left with three impossible directions: stop trusting any of her negative feelings, work harder to convince others that she is truly in a bad way, or hide the reality and keep faking it. Either way, there is no strengthening. Validation helps people experience that they are not making up a situation and thus are facing what truly is.

Assessing Reality

Attending also enables a person to assess the situation's realities. The group will often help by engaging the person in objective fact-finding. Sometimes they discover that the person isn't as weak or the situation as bad as he thought. The group strengthens by grounding the member in reality. For example, a wife might state that she can't talk to her husband about his drinking, because he will blow up at her and the kids. Then, as the group works with her, they find out that although he drinks too much, the husband has never blown up during their marriage. It is a fear she brings to the table. As she becomes aware of her fear, she is strengthened in her resolve to talk to her husband.

Internalizing External Structure

When there is true weakness and inability, however, the group functions somewhat like a cast on a broken limb. The limb is really broken and cannot operate or heal on its own. The cast becomes an external structure that protects and strengthens so that the limb can repair. In the same way, groups take over where the weak person gives out. They provide love, support, advice, and encouragement when the person just doesn't have the resolve to do something that seems difficult or even impossible (1 Thessalonians 5:14).

Suppose a member has a weight problem and cannot seem to get the time to work out. The desire is there, but life gets in the way. The person feels defeated and discouraged. The group may set up a phone arrangement so that she gets a call an hour before her exercise time. The calls strengthen her decision, ground her in what is really important, and help her break out of whatever distracts her at the time. The group helps her feel loved enough to take the right steps. She internalizes this strengthening from the members, making the experiences of support a part of her, until the time when she no longer needs the calls. The cast can be removed, and the limb can operate on its own.

Identification

Good groups also support and strengthen by identifying with failure. They understand that the person may continue to fail in a certain area until he is strong enough to move on. They remember going through that, too. People well acquainted with failure are the best at strengthening others. Jesus commanded Peter to "strengthen your brothers" (Luke 22:32) after he had failed miserably and had then been restored. True strengthening helps people face and accept failure as part of the growth process rather than being afraid of making mistakes. They strengthen each other through accepting, and then supporting, their members' weak parts. A person may say, "I have 'been there' with my wife, too, and I empathize with how lonely you feel."

Support and strengthening provide basic elements that help people survive and grow.

Chapter 12

Mentoring

I (John) am in small group that has met for many years. It is not arranged around any theme except spiritual and personal growth. We have experienced many landmarks together, such as marriages, children, moves, career changes, and losing loved ones.

The group changes focus according to what we perceive we need and are interested in. For example, sometimes we will formally study some biblical topic; other times, it will be a book on spiritual or personal matters. At times there has been no topic except what is going on in life. We know each other pretty well now, at many levels. The whole person is involved.

I am constantly aware that my group has mentored me in many areas of my life, such as marriage, parenting, devotional life, and work. They have guided and instructed me and have helped me grow and mature. I am grateful for the years and experiences of mentoring that the group has provided for me.

Evaluate Qualifications

All of us at some point in life can benefit from mentors, if we have the humility to defer to someone else's input and insight about us. There are three requirements. First, the mentors are qualified. That is, they have experience and competency in the area of concern. Second, they are safe people who care about us. Third, they know us well enough to help us. A good and healthy group can meet these requirements. Talk with the members about how to make the group a mentoring environment.

Bring the Whole Person into the Mentoring

When groups operate well, the entirety of each member becomes the subject, not just a part of the person. That is the nature of love and relationship, according to God's design. Love is about the whole person: "Love the Lord your God with all your heart and with all your soul and with all your mind and with all your strength" (Mark 12:30). This is the entire soul of the person: values, thoughts, behaviors, beliefs, emotions, moods, and attitudes.

Members continue to open up about all parts of themselves when the group is warm and interested. When a group deals with someone's issue or concern, it will also ask for context: how she got into her situation; past patterns; others' influence; weaknesses and strengths she brings to the problem. So the more the whole person is involved, the better the resolution of the issue. In turn, the member is more fully known by the group. This translates into a deeper relationship and more connection. Now the group is better able to assist that person in other areas of life because of what has happened up to the present.

The Process of Mentoring

The group can help a member develop experience, competency, and wisdom in some specific area of life. The other members share the burden of guidance and assist the member to grow in that area. For example, the group may help a newly married couple to develop responsible financial values early in the relationship. They may provide principles, advice, and resources and share their own experiences. Since they know the couple on a personal level, they may have valuable feedback to help them see what weak points to be aware of and deal with. They may help monitor the couple's growth and progress in that area over time. They coach, direct, train, and develop the couple so that the two people become strong and mature in their dealings with money.

This mentoring does not require a broadly structured group such as mine. In fact, a topically based group offer a great deal of guidance in the specific areas it is addressing. I have seen a parenting group, for example, help its members to establish a core approach to raising kids and develop a set of values and then address practical concerns that have brought great benefit to all involved.

Mentoring Begets More Mentoring

Trust builds up between the group and its members as they experience being safely loved, graced, and helped. People more easily open up parts of themselves and more freely expose areas of need. In a sense, the person goes to the group for guidance and growth in all the areas of life, because he has gained so much life from the group. That is what we mean by mentoring. Though the members are adults and treat each other as adults, the group shoulders some responsibility to be a support, guide, and path for the entire way of the person. The members become more of whom God created them to be because of the group mentoring. Help your members to be aware of their next mentoring step and bring it to the group. When groups mentor their members, they do their part to help each one become an adult in all the ways in which we are to grow up.

Chapter 13

Grieving

Loss happens. It is a sad but inevitable reality of life after the Fall. We lose people through death, divorce, geographic move, or alienation. We lose things in our own lives, such as careers, health, or opportunities. We must learn to deal with each loss in healing ways that promote growth and faith. Groups provide an invaluable help for people navigating through the dark, strange experience of any loss. Groups do this by helping their members work through the mourning process that God uses to help us resolve loss: "Blessed are those who mourn, for they will be comforted" (Matthew 5:4).*

Whether or not a small group chooses loss as a specific study topic, the nature of life ensures that *the longer people meet, the higher the chances are that someone will encounter a loss*. In addition, as groups grow

---

*For a fuller treatment of grief see our book *How People Grow* (Grand Rapids: Zondervan, 2001), chapter 11.

safer, people feel more permission to bring up past but unresolved losses.

Invite and Contain Sad, Confused, Angry Emotions

The group will allow the member not only to talk about the facts of the loss, but to experience the corresponding feelings. Loss involves a great deal of emotion. Generally speaking, the greater the loss, the greater the intensity and range of feelings. The group serves as a place where a person can safely feel how much she loves and misses the individual who is no longer around. This is especially valuable with people whose approach to loss has been to appear strong, get busy, look at the positives, and find other ways to mitigate how deeply they are bereft of another. The group is not afraid of sadness. It does not worry whether negative feelings are bad or dangerous. Instead, members use their own identifications with loss to help the struggler with hers.

Help the Person Go through the Stages of Grief

The group understands that grief over a loss has a movement and structure. People may deny reality, protest it, move into despair, and finally accept it fully and move back into life. The group is "with" the person during all these parts of the process. They empathize with whatever stage the member is in, and they help him move to the next level when he is ready. Their awareness that grief has an order to it allows them to help him not get stuck forever in his loss and pain. A group member might say, "I know a few weeks ago you were still in shock about the death in your family, but now it seems you are more protesting against its unfairness. I want to know more about this with you."

Allow a Process of Time to Pass

The group lets the person talk and feel what she needs to when she first brings up the issue. But it knows that she will in all likelihood need to address the loss in subsequent, perhaps many, group meetings. There will be times when the person is dealing with another, unrelated matter, then all of a sudden she moves back into the loss. This is part of the ebb and flow of grief. It allows a person to get involved in life's affairs. Then, when there is time, space, and enough support, the person again moves back into the sadness. At the same time, the group is aware that the process does have a direction to it, so that if the members notice that the person seems to have prematurely cut off things, they can bring it up and find out how she is doing. The issue may have been short-circuited due to her level of the pain, fears of draining the group, or the idea that she shouldn't still be so weak. The group helps her get back on track and stay on track.

Provide a Resource for Bearing Loss

The grieving member needs to replace what he has lost in order to resolve the matter. The group is a central source of whatever the person is now deprived of, such as love, stability, acceptance, structure, or a sense of belonging. When a group does not understand that they are to actually function as the resource the person has lost, sometimes the members become passive or somewhat uninvolved, thinking that being present and caring is about all they can supply. But the healthy group actually helps fill in the holes left by the one who is no longer present. As a result, the process moves along at its own pace. Members might say, "We are aware of how your dad was a strong and stabilizing person for you. I hope we can help there, too, as you go through the loss."

Teach a Stance on Grief and Loss

The group offers a great environment for members to go through life's losses thoroughly and well. It also helps people learn how to think about loss, what is involved, and their specific tasks and responsibilities regarding someone else's loss. Good groups are both a hospital and a training center to help people understand and be knowledgeable about loss.

Help with Faith

Ultimately, the group assists the grieving person by being the place where the struggler can come to terms with God. Grief often takes an individual through a period of questioning period God's provision, care, and place in loss. The group hears the questions and knows which ones to answer and which ones to simply be there for. Going through the grief process, with God and the group as supports and guides, often deepens and enriches an individual's faith. The group helps point him to, and trust the love of, Christ, who was "a man of sorrows, and familiar with suffering" (Isaiah 53:3). This is the final resolution, when the person can say good-bye with all his heart and move further into the good life that God has for him.

Chapter 14

Healing

One of a good group's main tasks is healing. At one level or another, every member comes to group bearing some sort of emotional or personal injury. That is, we are a wounded people, and we suffer from the wounds we bear, whether an unloved heart, a fear of conflict, or an inability to manage stress and struggle. The group is the ideal setting for gaining healing from these injuries, old and new.

When an individual brings up an issue, the group will in a sense circle around the wounded family member, as you will sometimes see a herd of animals do in the wild. All of their attention is focused on the one who is hurt. That is what is needed at this point in time.

Comfort the Hurting

When a person is hurt, the first thing a group does is to help bring comfort, care, and soothing. Talking about injuries brings along with it painful, distressing, and upsetting emotions, memories, and thoughts. The group takes on the task of "being there" when the person tells about her injurious experience. This action restores a sense of being loved, safe, and stable, which prepares the person to move further toward healing.

Validation

As we mentioned in the section on support and strengthening, good groups confirm the wounded person's emotional reality. That is, they let her know her experience matters, her feelings are real, and those feelings and experiences are important to them. Often, *the extent to which people heal from injuries is the extent to which others validate the injuries.* The group may have to persevere to overcome the message of invalidation the member received from others. Such messages made the sufferer nullify her own experience: *These things didn't happen to you, or they weren't as bad as you think.* But as the group provides support, the person becomes more confident that her injury is real and matters to others.

Assessment

The group also pays particular attention to helping the wounded member assess the nature and extent of his injuries, in preparation to help him heal. One important aspect is that the group helps the person *separate injury from symptom.* Most people are not aware of the difference, but it is significant. For example, depression or anxiety can be both painful symptoms and the results of certain injuries, among them emotional detachment, an inability to set limits, or harsh internal expectations. While the symptom is quite distressing, it functions as a red flag to the underlying injury. Good groups help the person assess what really causes the pain. A member might tell another, "I think I am understanding how bad the depression is, but I want you to talk about what is going on beneath it."

In addition, the group determines if it has proper resources for the injuries' extent and severity. There are times when a person's wounds need more structure, safety, intensity, or experience than the group can provide.

Strength to Take Ownership

Whether the injuries are other-inflicted, self-inflicted, or the result of living in an imperfect world, each person needs to take responsibility for his part in resolving things. The healthy group, while being full of grace, comfort, and validation, also helps the member to avoid a helpless victim stance, blaming others and remaining passive. Instead the group helps him shoulder the burdens he should. The group may say to the member, "We are on your side, and we agree that this is a bad situation. Now we want to help you do whatever it takes to be restored from this and be healed inside so that you are not prey to these situations ever again."

Emotionally Corrective Experiences

The group becomes a context for the member to engage in experiences that change thinking, heal wounds, and give strength and confidence. For example, the group may encourage the injured person to embrace some memory or pain and not avoid it; to take a risk and confront someone; to practice admitting the truth; or to risk failure and try again. These experiences, when surrounded by the group's love, support, and acceptance, help the member grow and heal. In this sense, God uses the group to repay the individual for what has been taken away, "for the years the locusts have eaten" (Joel 2:25).

It is probably obvious at this point that we believe that groups do much more than just help someone cope. Groups use the power that God provides to give people a new life, new ways of relating, and new ways to experience themselves. These signs are what healing is really all about.

Chapter 15

Confrontation

A group that is growing its members into maturity is a loving group. It is also a confronting group. That is, while it gives grace, it also speaks directly to and deals with hurtfulness and sin in its members. These can include deception, verbal attacks, controlling others, self-centeredness, all the way to affairs, financial indiscretions, or massive rebellions against the group's frame and structure.

An Integrated Approach

The best groups do not split up the tasks of grace and confrontation. In other words, they don't first offer a grace session and then have a confrontation session; that promotes emotional division within its members. *Instead, a good group gives love and support while simultaneously being clear about issues that must be confronted.*

This group function of confrontation is related to discipline and accountability, which have been addressed in their own chapters. None

are warm-fuzzy issues, because they deal with truth telling and directness. But confrontation is unique from these other two functions in that
it focuses more specifically on how to correct someone in the right way
and how sin is dealt with. Most people don't come into a group with a
healthy idea of how either should work. The second family helps model
it and provides members with a real-life template.

How to Practice Confrontation

The following five guidelines explain how a good group can incorporate confrontation into its growth process:

Normalize and expect confrontation and truth. The group constantly makes truth telling a safe, helpful, and expected part of its meetings. It reinforces people's courage to confront each other in healthy
ways. It also confronts those who are not doing any confronting. The
group doesn't interpret passivity, people pleasing, or rescuing as growth
behaviors, but as problems to be resolved. Most significantly, in a good
group members learn, session by session, that confrontation is not the
catastrophic event they have feared or even truly experienced. No one
gets out of control, has a tantrum, or gets harmed. Rather, people "truth"
each other in love and then move on to some other topic or person without a major disruption of the relationships and love. This is a new and
integrative experience for many members.

Address patterns more than events. A good group understands the
proper time to address something. It does not take on a policing stance,
confronting a member every time she does anything wrong. Rather, it
is aware of recurring patterns that cause obvious problems in the person,
group, or member's outside relationships. It is very important to deal
with such problems in the group context. For example, if Tracy interrupts someone's discussion, let it go. If Tracy continues to do so, the
group members might say, "Tracy, I don't know if you are aware of this,
but in the last several meetings you haven't let people finish their
thoughts. Can we talk about this?"

No condemnation and no equivocation. The group confronts as a
family made up of broken and healing sinners, not as an angry judge or

perfect parent: "Brothers, if someone is caught in a sin, you who are spiritual should restore him gently. But watch yourself, or you also may be tempted" (Galatians 6:1). Members are not harsh or condemning, because they know how much grace they themselves need. They know how judgment breaks and causes them to withdraw from the support they need.

At the same time, the group is direct and not ambiguous about the concern. They explain why the problem matters to them and the person. The member should know clearly what the group sees as a problem and how it affects them. Though the group is "for" the person, they have something "against" her, in the same way that Jesus had some things "against" his followers (Revelation 2:4, 14, 20).

Invitation to redemption. As the group speaks directly about the issue, it also entreats its member to confess, repent, and be restored to them. The group takes a stance that the sin gets in the way of a growing relationship with God and them, and they want it resolved so that the closeness can continue. Sometimes the group's invitation to redemption is enough. The person realizes how important she is to the group and gives up the behavior or attitude. This is not the end, as sins often require some digging and healing. But it begins the process of allying people's hearts to all work on the issue with the same mind.

Containment. This term refers to how the group addresses the problem or sin, understands the member's point of view, offers support and resources, and yet sets appropriate boundaries or consequences. In a way, the group quarantines the sin so that it cannot be hidden or ignored, but instead scrutinized and limited. Problems remaining beyond the person's control, even with group help, require more intensive resources. In matters of rebellion and willfulness, the group may have to be quite strict, to the point of asking the member to leave the group. Hopefully, though, following the tasks described above will get through to the member. The group's love, level of attachment, and clarity in confrontation, and the member's openness to God and reality, will usually solve the problem.

Chapter 16

Modeling

During my clinical psychology internship, I (John) worked at a children's day treatment center, where kids received intensive clinical help all day, five days a week, for several weeks. Something I experienced there helped me tremendously in working with people. At the end of the day, the kids and staff all formed a circle to review the day. Any person had the right to praise or confront another one on his behavior that day. If it was a confrontation, the recipient was not allowed to defend, excuse, or deny. He or she just had to take it. If it wasn't true, a staff member would correct it.

I watched five-year-olds tell teenagers, "Frank, you were really mean to me and Rachel, and it bothered me a lot." Then other kids would chime in and agree. It would "get to" the distant and rebellious teen in a way that staff confrontations could not. The teen would respond and change as a result, sometimes dramatically.

When my wife and I began our family, I remembered the healthy confrontation I'd seen modeled. We made that approach part of our family talks. Each member could praise or confront other family members, as long as it was true, and the other members, be they kids or adults, had to respond in nondefensive and humble ways. This approach has helped my family, my thinking about growth issues, and how I conduct groups.

A Picture of Growth

My experiences in the children's treatment center and my family are examples of how groups model good things for their members. The term *model* means *to imitate or conform to a chosen standard.* That is, the group provides a living, breathing picture for its members in various aspects of personal, relational, or emotional life. It fleshes out concepts, ideas, and conversations. When a group models, it gives its members something to experience and then internalize or make part of themselves.

Many people have told me how significant modeling was for them in their groups. Some had had no experience of how to conduct relationships or resolve problems. Others had bad, negative, or crazy experiences. So they had real struggles in getting through their outside lives until they saw the themes dealt with in healthy ways in the group.

Here are a few of the things a good group will model for its members:

- Vulnerability
- Need and dependency on each other
- Support
- Listening well
- Accepting failure
- Confessing faults so as to be restored
- Giving and receiving the truth
- Resolving conflict without ruining relationships
- Discerning people's character
- Forgiveness

The list could go on, but these important aspects of life are not just taught, but also caught, in the modeling tasks.

A Modeling Group Is Not a Perfect Group

Some people feel a demand or expectation that they be ideal or perfect as a model. This puts unrealistic pressure on a group. Also, a member who expects her group to be without blemish must lovingly be disabused of that notion. The best modeling, as indicated in the above list, is how *an imperfect group with imperfect members engages in the processes that ultimately heal them and grow them up.* Then the group is using "real people" with "real problems" to show each other how to deal redemptively with all their flaws and weaknesses.

The Members' "Two Selves"

Group members will find that they have two ways of relating in terms of modeling—"two selves." That is, they are both participant and observer. As the former, they will be part of some experience that the group models—for example, supporting someone who has an impossible child-rearing problem. As observer, they will review what they saw and learned as to how it may apply to their own situation. In this way there is a constant flow between watching how the group works with its members and being part of the process itself. This is how the best and most profound life change happens, when we both see and experience with others.

Modeling is often not so much an intentional group act as it is something that just occurs. Health and growth in a group beget health and growth in its members.

Chapter 17

Acceptance of Weakness

My life has not been a straight line. It has had many potholes and restarts. For example, after I (John) graduated from college, I moved a thousand miles away from home and college and worked for a couple of years in a children's home as a cottage parent. It was a high-stress job, and I really didn't have the maturity to manage it. I became burnt out, lonely, and depressed. Finally, in a phone call to my parents about this misery, they invited me to move back home and get my life together.

Initially I hated the idea, as it seemed like stepping backward. However, I couldn't see a better option, so I packed up and moved back. I got a job as a shoe salesman and began trying to figure out what to do when I grew up.

It was a weird time for me, as many of the friends I had grown up with had stayed in town, and their life paths were working for them. They were advancing in their careers, establishing themselves, marrying, and buying houses. I found out about all this as I sold them their shoes.

A Lifeline

At the same time, I became involved in a spiritual growth group of people my age. They wanted to grow in faith and personal relationships. We met regularly to talk, hang out, study the Bible, and pray.

In a nutshell, that group became a lifeline for me. I settled down and stabilized. They didn't care that I thought of myself as this total loser who couldn't make it in the real world. They didn't see me that way, yet they didn't try to talk me out of my own experience, either. They listened to my complaints and dreams. They confronted my unhelpful attitudes, and they gave me wise advice and feedback.

Gradually, as I began to grow and change in the group, a path began to appear in my head. It wasn't really through any group member's suggestion. Rather, it emerged as we all talked about our lives. The path became a growing awareness and desire to get formally trained in theology at a seminary, with the eventual goal of some sort of ministry. I believe that is how God led me in those dark days. I finally left home again for good. I entered seminary and eventually trained to be a psychologist.

I always look back at that group and those folks as helping me do a makeover in life. They were there, they cared, they got involved with me, and they spoke the truth. For me, they were a model of what group should be like. I learned how powerful and effective groups can be, in actually changing our insides, our values, our attitudes, and the entire course of our lives. In other words, the small group is not just about getting together to learn and connect, though it certainly does that. It is also about being involved in God's makeover process for all of us. He is there and present in such groups, and he is ready to help you in whatever restart you need. Let us look at a key characteristic of groups ready for life-changing growth.

Accepting Inability

As facilitator you must help members understand that *the demands of reality are greater than the members' ability to meet them.* This is simply the human condition. Life demands many tasks—doing a job well, finding a career path, finding or developing or holding onto a relationship, raising a family, and controlling our behavior. These aren't unrealistic demands. They are simply a part of life and a reason we all need grace.

At the same time, all of us have weaknesses, inabilities, or frailties that serve as obstacles to what life requires. These weaknesses are frustrating. They are our problem and no one else's. For example, some people cannot make emotional connections and thus are deprived of a necessary source of motivation and strength. Others cannot focus on and execute tasks. Still others are easily controlled by significant relationships in their lives. Some have a discouraging habit or addiction that prevents investing in what they really want out of life.

All these and more prove to us that no matter how hard we try, how much willpower we muster up, we can't pull off life the way we need to. As the Bible teaches, we do what we don't want to, and we don't do what we want to (Romans 7:14–21). There is a large gap between what we are expected to be and do and what we really are and do.

Instead of pretending this gap of inability does not exist, a group should develop a culture among its members that helps them accept the gap. In fact, *the gap is a large part of the reason people are in the group.* Though members initially bring fear and shame into the group, hiding their inability, the meetings should celebrate that we are all in the same condition.

As a facilitator you will see people say things like, "I should be able to keep my temper with my toddler, but . . ." or "I really want to find a decent relationship, but I attract the wrong people." People enter your group with the conviction that they shouldn't have the struggles they are having.

Your job is to help the members understand that God's grace and help are received best when people realize they are unable. They need him, cry out for mercy, and ask for help. That is how God works: "Blessed are the poor in spirit, for theirs is the kingdom of heaven" (Matthew 5:3). Tell them, "You are right. You can't do these things that are important to do in life. Neither can I, and that's basically a membership requirement for being here. You and your inability are welcome here."

This is a very important stance to develop, as new members often expect that they are the only ones with struggles or need only a few tips to be on their way. Worst of all, they worry that if they reveal how bad things are inside, other people will not be able to handle them. So they come ready and willing to act strong and able when, in reality, they are hurting and failing. The good group instead helps members understand that inability is the condition of all.

Furthermore, a good group conveys hope for the members to resolve and fix the inability gap. Growing in groups is not about coping, managing, and staying the same. It is about being in God's process of transformation and lifelong change. Group provides help, resources, love, wisdom, and strengthening to help with whatever a person cannot do. What one person has been unable to pull off, several people can help her do. So let her know that, while all members experience the gap, things can and do change profoundly. That's how God's process works.

As a leader, you can help your group develop this stance toward inability:

- Model failure as normal
- Invite people to talk safely about their inability
- Help the group to move toward those who acknowledge weakness
- Confront the pretense of having it all together

Give examples of how your own life changed because people gave you what you didn't possess.

Chapter 18

Discipleship

The term *disciple* means pupil or learner. In the Old Testament it also refers to *one who is accustomed to something*. These definitions describe well a significant part of what groups do in their members' lives. That is, groups help individuals become learners of God's ways by getting them accustomed, or acclimated, to righteous ways of living and relating. Through many types of experiences, groups engage their people to show now that God's ways are best.

Pointing Members toward God

Thus, a growing group will direct its members toward God, his resources, and his biblical principles. All these hold the power, guidance, and help members need to heal and mature. The group points its members to God as their source. It shows them that personal growth, relational growth, and emotional growth are all spiritual growth. The laws and realities that help people grow come from God as their foundation, as we illustrate in *How People Grow.* When members understand the spiritual nature of these processes and see that the Bible contains the needed principles, they understand that they are being discipled and led in growth.

A Life Based on God's Values

Groups model and teach their people by word and by experience that the things important to God work best for us. They show their members that living in loving, intimate relationship helps their lives. Groups help members experience the freedom that comes with being honest and taking ownership over their lives. Groups instruct members that by being real and authentic, they have better connections, solve problems better, and achieve their desired goals. Discipleship happens because the great laws are not only true, but work in profound ways in the group and in a member's life.

Healing and Maturing

Sometimes people are confused about the nature of a group: Is it recovery? growth? discipleship? Often, terms such as *recovery* and *healing* refer to the process of addressing broken parts of a person's life, while *growth* and *discipleship* are used more in the context of moving toward maturity. There are good group contexts that specialize in these processes and uniquely contribute to spiritual growth. However, in any type of healthy group, these lines become a little blurry. A group of people who want to become disciples of Christ must also deal with their hurts and injuries. This frees them up to know him and make him known in even more meaningful ways. At the same time, those who want to recover from habits, pasts, and relationships that imprison them must also engage in the process of growth. Thus, discipleship is a part of any good and growing group.

One of the most fulfilling experiences for me is to take leaders through growth group processes. These are people whom God has called and gifted to head up some arena of life. Yet when they allow the group to take them through their own hurt and brokenness, and disciple them, their ministries and organizations often grow in ways and to levels that they had never dreamed of.

An Environment for Hunger

When the group disciples its members, it develops within them a desire and hunger for more information, growth, and good experiences. Members see so much more to be learned and known. They are encouraged to go out into their outside lives and integrate grace, truth, and growth into all contexts of their world. Most of all, groups show members that growth is about more than solving a problem, pain, or relational conflict. Those things may have triggered the discipleship journey, but the path is much more comprehensive and deeper than anything they have ever experienced. Members can tell each other, "I am glad you are finding answers in your parenting, but I want to encourage you to bring other areas of your life to the group also."

Giving Back

In this same vein, the group creates within its members a desire to help others with what they have learned and experienced. Disciples are sent to a world of broken people who need God, his redemption, and his ways. Their lives, influences, and ways of loving give birth in others to what they have found in the group's processes. An example of fostering this might be, "Jay, now that you've been so much more open with the group, I want to hear how this openness is affecting those in your outside life." Sometimes the Jays reach out directly to others in their neighborhood or work.

I have seen this kind of fostering happen literally as groups birth other groups. The tasks are the same, and those who have been healed and discipled bring those experiences and teachings to others who need them. In this way, small groups play a large role in helping to promote God's kingdom: "Therefore go and make disciples of all nations, baptizing them in the name of the Father and of the Son and of the Holy Spirit, and teaching them to obey everything I have commanded you. And surely I am with you always, to the very end of the age" (Matthew 29:19–20).

PART 3

STARTING A SMALL GROUP

Chapter 19

Decide on the Purpose and Type of Group

As you design your small group, you will want to explore a second issue by yourself and with people who have experience in these matters. It is the issue of balancing *process versus structure,* sometimes referred to as *experience versus truth.* However framed, it addresses fundamental issues of what makes a group a group and how groups can best be designed.

If your group structure and design have already been created and developed, this may not be an immediate question. As you grow in your experience, interest, and confidence in facilitating a group, you will want to investigate other ways to do this in your growth adventure.

The Two Threads

Small groups incorporate two threads that intertwine throughout meeting times: truth/structure and process/experience. The first thread involves the group's structural makeup, such as how ordered the group is and how it imparts truth to its members. The second involves process elements, that is, how much emotional closeness and experiences are right for the group.

There is no right or wrong. It has more to do with the group's nature and needs, the elements of which we present here. However, it is true that *for a group to be a group, you need some amount of both.* If a group has no process, it is more of a teaching class, whose goal is to provide helpful information about a topic. If it has no truth or structure, it could be a backyard barbecue: no agenda, but a lot of fun hanging out.

Years ago, when Henry and I designed and conducted groups for our inpatient programs, we adopted a model that involved many different types of group settings. However, the core of the program was built around two specific groups. The first was a didactic, or teaching, group in which a clinician would lecture on a spiritual or emotional growth topic, such as what the Bible teaches about relationship, the nature of emotional disorder, or our hiding styles. The patients would take notes, ask questions, and work on understanding the material. The second type of group, conducted by a therapist and called a process group, had no agenda except what the patients brought up. Here they either dealt with their own issues and relationships or gave a personal response to what they'd learned from the didactic group. So, daily during this intensive stay, people were involved in truth and structure as well as process and experience. They used both threads to heal and grow.

Your group can mix these two elements, depending on its goals. For example, *discipleship small groups* are designed to help members learn fundamental doctrines and discover how to follow God. These groups are higher in structure and lower in process, as they have a body of knowledge to convey in a given amount of time. *Process groups* have no agenda but helping people with whatever is going on in their lives. These may open with silence, and people begin however they wish, in a low-structure, high-process fashion. The goal of *seeker-type groups* is to provide a safe place for nonbelievers and believers to interact. For example, a seeker group structured around discussing movies people have seen would be more process-based and open-ended.

Henry and I produce material that mixes both elements. It has a built-in structure concerning a topic, such as relationships, marriage, parenting, or dating. The leader simply uses but does not have to create the materials or structure. We also provide discussion and process sections to help the group members connect with each other on deeper levels.

We describe the two elements below, after which we suggest ways to decide on the mix you may want for your own small group.

The Truth/Structure Aspect

The truth/structure aspect includes the elements of safety, valuable information, and a springboard into internalization.

A study guide, manual, workbook, or topic provides members with a certain amount of predictability that makes them feel safe, if they need that. They know the group will have some sort of order. This is why many groups begin with a topic and then move into personal discussion.

Good-quality formal content is proven, because it helps people grow. Biblically based principles provide a path for understanding issues, answers, and hope.

Well-designed study materials also help members become curious about their own experiences and contexts, which moves them into the process element. People use the information as a means of coming to know themselves, group members, and God better.

The Process/Experience Aspect

The process/experience aspect recognizes growth as a part of life, grasped through relationships. Members share themselves as whole people and become more aware.

When they understand growth material as a part of life, members move into their hearts and inner lives. The truths become real and alive to them. They begin to grasp growth in terms of relationships, not simply ideas. One of the most powerful elements of change in a group happens through what psychologists call the "I-thou" aspect of personal growth—when people talk *to each other about their experience of each other*. For example, when a person opens up about his isolation and internal emptiness and can confess, "I need to know that you are here with me in this," he and the others are profoundly affected.

The whole person becomes known as all thoughts, feelings, values, attitudes, behaviors, and losses are welcomed. The person is brought into the group with heart, soul, and mind.

Members learn awareness on a personal level. They see how they affect others and how others affect them, which leads to change. For example, a woman may hear from a member, "Kim, when you enter into the process, it always seems to become about you. I don't mean to sound bugged, but I would like it to be more mutual between us." Kim may find that this long-term pattern has affected all her significant relationships; her awareness helps her change. In addition to the "I-thou" process, people process their own lives, experiences, and feelings or responses to the content or material. In that way the group helps to process the very content they studied. Content and process meet.

Determining the Mix

As you fit the process/structure mix to your group goals, remember to work from the ideal and be sensitive for newer groups' need for structure. You will also want to consider your members' interest in specific content, functioning level, and dynamics during meetings.

Ideally, good content provides a foundation from which insight, feelings, experiences, connections, and growth flow. The process elements then create the deepest and longest-lasting life changes.

New facilitators and new groups will, as a rule, need more structure and content, less process and experience. These provide a safe surrounding to enter the world of a group environment. Conversely, with more time and experience a group may be able to do with less structure as it becomes internalized and members trust the group process.

Some groups want to delve into a particular topic such as parenting, communication, or conflict resolution. In these cases, more content is warranted.

The lower the members' functioning level, the greater their need for structure. People in crisis, serious recovery, or deep loss or with chronic debilitating emotional issues need more structure to keep them stable and safe. Those who may feel and experience distress and pain but are able to meet the demands of work, family, and relationships can do with less structure.

As a facilitator you need to be aware of how people's feelings and reactions—especially negative emotions—shift during the group time itself. For example, study material may provoke hurt or sadness in a member. Or a member may come to the group feeling distressed from a situation in her outside life. You may notice pronounced, unresolved tension between members. This may be the time to give up content for process, because the members probably already know it's going on, and nobody can really attend to the material till you deal with the issue.

For example, you may want to say, "Beth, it seems you are really upset right now. How about if we lay aside the materials for now and talk about what's going on?" Valuable group time may occur as Beth opens up.

Monitor this, however. If a group cannot get through a lesson without getting derailed, make that a topic of discussion. You may find that someone needs more processing time than the group offers or more resources than the group has. Maybe the materials aren't engaging the members, or perhaps they want more process time in general.

Ultimately, the mix you determine will be a reflection of life itself as you daily hear the truth and experience its meaning in your lives.

Design the Group Purpose and Type

Over the past few years, the leadership in my own church has invested heavily into transforming itself into becoming a church of small groups. As part of that value I recently signed on to lead a group of junior high boys. (I know—what was I thinking, right?) During our leadership training we were given lots of room to be creative and design our group the way we felt best. So I played with different models and types and finally came up with a basic design. We start off with a little "what's going on with everybody" part, then we have a brief interactive Bible lesson on a topic they want to deal with, such as girls or dysfunctional parents. Next we discuss problems and pray for each other. I have enjoyed talking to the other group leaders, who lead the same type of kids yet use various designs. Some groups incorporate physical activities such as relay races and Frisbee throwing; some focus on family matters; some learn theology and Bible memory. All the kids seem to be flourishing. I keep thinking how different my life would have been if I had been in one of these groups during junior high.

Start with Reconciliation

As a group facilitator you may be in a program that has a comprehensive, developed structure. You may be free to determine, within certain parameters such as recovery or twelve-step, what kind of group you want. Or you may have a blank screen, in which you can choose whatever design you think best. Even if you are in the first category, it helps to think through group design and purpose issues so that you can understand, use, and modify things as you gain more experience.

Most important, always begin with the transcendent purpose that all small groups share—*the ministry of reconciliation*, as we described in chapter 2. Your job is to bring people back to God and the kind of life he created them for (2 Corinthians 5:18–20). God seeks, saves, and grows his people in that reconciliation process. That is your anchor, the place you can always return to for clarity and direction.

Purpose and Type

Reconciliation takes many shapes and forms in church and small group life. That is why it helps to think through your group's purpose and type. What do you want to accomplish? What functions and tasks should the group perform? Some facilitators have been deeply touched in their own growth by certain types of groups; they believe in that group type's power because of what has happened in their own lives. These are important matters, not only for you, but for the group. The clearer your group is on its design purpose, the better will be the members' buy-in. Conversely, this also helps determine who would not be interested in or appropriate for the group.

Here are a few general examples of group purpose and design. These are not technical and precise, and there are more types than these:

Bible/book study members meet to study various passages or books in the Bible or books about biblical topics. They concentrate on understanding and applying the truths and praying for and supporting each other.

Topical support group members meet regarding a specific area of interest or growth such as marriage, parenting, dating, or relationships. They study materials geared toward the topic and relate to each other regarding the subject.

Recovery group members come together to heal from an area of struggle such as addictions, bad habits, divorce, or codependent relationships. They often have a twelve-step structure, as does Saddleback Church's Celebrate Recovery program.

General support or growth group members meet to grow spiritually, emotionally, and personally. They bring their daily lives, interests, and struggles to bear in the meeting.

Don't get lost in the details of the format, however. Keep uppermost in mind the lives and needs of the individuals you are preparing to spend some hours and weeks with, face to face and life to life.

Other Determining Factors

Other factors determining the nature of your small group include your calling, others' needs, leadership perceptions, and available time.

What is your calling and passion? Has God given you a heart for a particular ministry or situation? Some people find themselves repeatedly drawn back to a certain design. At the same time, don't confuse passion with comfort zone. Sometimes it is good to stretch yourself into new group designs.

Ultimately the group's "second family" function is to serve its members' needs. What spiritual, emotional, personal, or relational needs do you want to see met?

What do the church leaders who recruited you perceive as most important in designing a small group? How do they see your contribution?

You should also consider your available time and resources. Before choosing the type of group you want to lead, look at your own experience in growth matters and evaluate how much you can invest in a group.

Members' emotional and spiritual needs are more important than group design or format. Your group type need not be set in stone. Often, as a leader experiences different settings, she will find a different model works better. The more varied the experiences, the better. Adapt the structure to what is best for members, not the reverse. Just as the Sabbath was made for man's good and not the opposite (Mark 2:27), so the group should be designed for its members' good.

Leave the results to God. While designing your small group, it is easy to slip into taking on responsibility for the fruits in its prospective members' lives. Let that burden rest with the members and God, where it belongs; they will ultimately determine how much growth, healing, and benefit comes. Your job is to provide a good set of elements that, if used, can cause growth. Love the members, be involved, have good structure and materials, know how to interact on a personal level, and jump in.

Chapter 20

Choose Study Materials

I f you spend time in Christian bookstores, you have probably noticed that there is no shortage of group materials. It is a fortunate time to be alive, when it seems people are becoming excited about the small group concept and the pipeline is being filled with material. This chapter provides direction for you, as the facilitator, to wade into the sea of information to choose your topic and materials. It also helps you establish a framework and communicate its importance to the group.

Choosing Your Topic

People's needs come first not only in determining your group's purpose and design, but also in choosing your topic.

People come first. When choosing the topic, look first at people's needs for growth. What do they struggle with, desire, or have interest in? People give up other things to make room for the groups they sign up for. Ask the people who recruited you about the needs they sense. Get very important feedback from members themselves. If you know them personally, look at what is going on in their lives.

Talking with members new to small groups will help you understand their needs, while experience may give you perspective on what can help meet those needs. For example, people who struggle with poor relationships may want to study why others can be such jerks, while you might want them to look at why they are drawn to the wrong people!

Topics change as people change. You are not locked forever into a content area. If the attachments are good and people are getting something out of the group, the topics may change as lives change. My group has studied several different topics, depending on what was going on in our lives—relating to God, reading classic Christian mystics, marriage principles, and so forth. We have also had topic-less seasons in which we just wanted to be in each others' presence and open up our lives to each other.

You will also want to figure out how long to stay on a topic. Some studies last four to six weeks, which is probably a minimum for effectiveness. Some, like Bible Study Fellowship, go on for years. In a church where several hundred people use our Foundations series curriculum every week, group members go through the material in about a year and then start over again. The leaders perceive that as people grow, they change enough in a year to reuse the same principles at new and deeper levels. This pattern has been going on for several years. Make sure everyone is on the same page in this regard, because some people like to try lots of things to find out where they should land, while others are ready to commit to an in-depth, long-term study.

Broader may be better. The broader the topic, the more room people have to delve into other aspects of their lives and integrate them into the group meeting. For example, topics on spiritual and personal growth would tend to invite anything a person deals with, more than parenting topics would. If, however, the specific topic is where the need is, defer to that.

Your relationship to the content. Determine whether the topic is a good fit for you and where you are. Has the topic touched your life, and have you seen God's grace change you in that area? Is it still a new and raw topic, one you may not yet be ready to facilitate? Is it one you just can't feel any interest or passion about? The best fits are those the facilitator has enough experience with to have gained some wisdom and victory in the process.

Selecting Materials

The following seven guidelines will help you select appropriate material to meet your group's needs.

Biblical and sane. Technically, these terms are redundant because God is the author of sanity. However, just because study materials include Bible verses does not mean they are conveying God's meaning. Cults have been built on the strategy of using Scripture the wrong way. So check out the materials yourself and have experienced people look them over, too.

Recommended. Find people who have successfully led groups for a long time and ask them about materials. Their experiences will have taught them a wealth of knowledge about what works and what doesn't.

Created by those in the know. Look at the credentials of the authors of the materials. If the study guides involve process and group interaction, what is their training in group dynamics? If it is biblical content, are they qualified in their training and experience? Some people may not have much formal training, but the school of experience and a good track record have qualified them. Others may have both.

Has substance. It is important that the material go beyond the obvious solution of "do what you're supposed to do." As we mention elsewhere, good and growing groups do more than just read the Ten Commandments and stop. Choose substantive study guides that deal with the underlying causes, motives, injuries, values, misunderstandings, sins, failures, and weaknesses that impede growth. Look for materials that offer real hope and solutions.

Treats members as adults. Make sure the study materials take positions where the Bible takes positions—as on divorce or ethics—yet leave the same room and freedom that the Bible leaves for people to make choices. For example, you may choose several ways of "speaking the truth in love" (Ephesians 4:15) to your teen: tone of voice, environment and setting, the topics you bring up. Avoid materials that instruct you to use their exact words or rigid rules to convey something to your kid.

Practical. Concepts and principles need to be easily translated into application. Many study materials have homework or thought questions. These help to put flesh on the skeleton ideas being taught.

Fitting for the group nature. The type of people in your group may help you decide on materials. Often, if a group settles into itself over time, the members will want to venture out beyond formal group study guides. They may want to go over a topic or book they like and will undertake creating the study structure themselves. This great exercise in ownership can really motivate group members.

Pray and keep an open mind as you search out topics and materials. It is an exciting part of the process.

Chapter 21

Design the Frame

To establish group cohesion—a great indicator of group effectiveness—it is important to maintain a *frame* for the group. It is a little like a boundary that holds it all together. A frame structures the meeting frequency and beginning and ending times. It states attendance requirements, ground rules, and the like. The frame communicates to members how serious everyone is about the group.

Different Frames for Different Groups

The frame depends on what kind of group you lead. Some very open groups have no attendance requirement; with Alcoholics Anonymous, an open recovery group, anyone can come at any time and whenever they wish. On the other end of the spectrum, some groups decide to close membership for a time and want everyone to be there. Since it is closed and group membership is fixed, attendance is more vital. Other groups are somewhere in between. Obviously, there are valid reasons for missing a meeting, like illness or earthquakes, but in general, high commitment to attendance yields greater group cohesion and results.

Research shows that *prepared group members have much better outcomes than those who are not prepared to understand the structure, ground rules, and expectations.* Prepared members have more faith in the process and more participation along the way. This remains true over time, not just in the beginning. So if you want your members to do their part, to show up and participate, you will do well to train them about the group and orient them to your expectations about attendance and the frame.

Decide if you will be in charge of the frame or allow the group to have a say. When churches conduct groups through a particular ministry program, the program overseer sets the frame. For example, the overseer might say, "Our groups meet every Wednesday night for two hours. For the first half hour, a member or visiting speaker teaches a lesson. We spend the remaining ninety minutes processing the talk as it relates to our lives. We begin at seven-thirty and end at nine-thirty."

In other groups, members have some input about times, rules, and frequency. All contribute to the structure and decide as a group how to operate and define rules and consequences. It is up to you and the group to enforce these.

Communicating the Frame So Members Comply

Members are more likely to comply with the structure when you communicate its importance. Tell them first of all what the frame is, and then talk about why it is important. You might cover the following talking points:

- "We have all taken time away from busy lives to be here, so let's value each other's commitment by getting here and beginning on time. I will always begin the group on time, so if you are here, you won't miss anything. We will also end on time to respect the other things that everyone has going on."
- "Would some of you share whether you've experienced groups where people have not respected others' time and commitment? What are your feelings about attendance, punctuality,

and their importance? If anyone expects to have a problem with these issues, we'd like to know and plan for it."

- "Have you ever had a problem along those lines? If you do, how can we help you best?"
- "Let's talk together [if this is not in the rules] about what the group wants to do if someone is often late or misses lots of sessions. What is the consensus? Do you want to address it with each other as a group when you begin to feel it is distracting? Do you want to set a number of occurrences as a guideline that says when we bring it up? I think that if we don't agree ahead of time, we might all feel a little weird at the time, not knowing how to handle it. Maybe we can all get on the same team here now. We can do everything from ignoring tardiness or absenteeism to saying the late person buys everyone dinner! But it would be good to just make sure we are all on the same page."

You can use your own creativity and the group's to address this issue. What we suggest, however, is that you communicate to the members the importance of the frame and their responsibility to it. If you do that, you will make overt what everyone feels and wonders about covertly and, in doing so, give it value as well as a structure to deal with non-compliance.

Chapter 22

Select Members

Who is in a group can make the experience highly fruitful or unhelpful. One of the leader's most important tasks is picking the right group members. At the same time, don't think that this is a crystal ball; people have their own choices, paths, and even parts of themselves that no one knows about. But in the main, the more appropriate members create the better group experiences.

Finding Out about Potential Members

To determine the appropriateness of inviting a potential member, you can gain information in various ways, depending on your situation:

- Ask whether the *leadership* in your church or organization has already accomplished this through a screening or interview process.
- Seek information from *other people* who are in a position to know, such as a leader, a pastor, or a counselor.

- Find out whether the structure will train you and other facilitators in a simple *interview* process for gaining information.
- Check whether leaders want you to tell prospective members that the *initial meetings* are a trial balloon and they will be talked with afterward as to whether the group is right for them. This will help you as group facilitator to experience things you can't really find out in an interview.

Screening for What Is Appropriate

These avenues of information can also help you screen a potential member's appropriateness according to whether the group purpose fits the person's purpose and whether she has the appropriate values and abilities.

Group Purpose Fits Individual's Purpose

Each group should be designed with its own function and purpose, be it general spiritual growth, recovery, divorce issues, or whatever. Obviously, *the direction each individual wants to take should match the direction the group wants to take.* Make sure each prospective member understands what the group is to be about and that this purpose is of value and interest to him. This means the facilitator must be clear in her own thinking about the group's purpose so she can clearly articulate it to the prospective member.

Group Structure Fits Individual's Values and Abilities

Beyond the topic, however, make sure the prospective members understand what a group is about and how it operates. The principles and ideas of this book provide a blueprint for this discussion. One suggestion is to make sure the prospective member understands that the group involvement requires commitment to certain values and abilities for fulfilling these commitments.

We suggest that members be committed to:

The frame. As stated earlier, everyone should buy in and adapt to the group structure.

Attachments. Everyone should be willing to engage emotionally with other people on a heart level. Sometimes, due to his own injuries, a person will be unable to engage on an emotional level. Discuss such findings with your leader to determine whether the group is the right fit for each person.

Honesty. Groups work according to members' abilities to be as honest as possible. This doesn't mean a person never makes mistakes, but it does mean he endeavors to tell the truth as he perceives it and does not engage in deceptive or dishonest patterns.

Caring for others. Group members need to understand that caring for others' situations is as important as dealing with their own and they have to operate that way. Group is different from individual counseling: the person not only tolerates that not all interventions are about her, but she also benefits from the interaction. If, however, she cannot engage with the group as a whole but, for example, focuses only on the leader, you may need to reevaluate.

Receiving feedback. Good group members see the life-giving value of hearing the truth about ourselves from others. This last point is very important. Some group settings offer no feedback, or cross-talk, and such groups have value in and of themselves for their own missions. At the same time, we believe that giving and receiving feedback, when done safely, is one of the most growth-producing elements of a group. Clearly state the value of feedback. If you don't, you risk someone feeling betrayed or blindsided: "I just wanted a support group; I didn't come here to be criticized," even though the feedback was right on. Make sure prospective group members don't carry a "womb" picture of the group as a place where people only support and empathize. Make sure they know the group will also lovingly confront and challenge them.

Besides being committed to these five values, the prospective group members need the ability to work within the values. Whether the person is appropriate for your group may depend on the following issues:

Clinical issues. The person may be dealing with a diagnosed issue such as depression, anxiety, panic attacks, or eating disorders. This does not mean he isn't right for your group; it does mean you need to deal with it. Go to your leadership and ask what procedure they have adopted to address this aspect.

Ideally, if the person is getting treatment from a qualified clinician (therapist), a group can be an invaluable support to their work. However, it is sometimes important for the person to find out whether the clinician thinks group membership is okay. You could even ask the person, or in some situations the therapist, how the group might help with the member's therapeutic goals.

Ability to deal with regression and conflict safely. Because groups can be emotionally intense, the person needs the internal ability to experience regression (emotions and perspectives from the past) as well as conflict with other members. A person who is right for the group can engage in these safely, recover fairly quickly, and use the experience to grow. When, however, someone is unable to come out of the experience or it constantly causes him or the group great disruption, it may be appropriate to switch the person to a setting with more structure, safety, or expertise. Their needs may be beyond your purpose or skills.

Present crisis. Going through a divorce, severe parenting crisis, or medical emergency does not at all rule out a prospective member, but the crisis should be discussed. Are they able to deal with their crisis and still engage mutually in the group? Would a group that deals specifically with their crisis be a better match?

Functioning level. Function refers to how well the person deals with life in general: keeping a job or career, maintaining significant family and friendship relationships, having a relatively stable life. Generally, the more similar the members' functioning levels, the better. At the same time, don't allow that similarity to create a cliquey feeling in the group. Confront any sense of entitlement you see in the group.

Variance. Groups in which everyone is the same sometimes get stuck. Allow different sorts of people and perspectives to join. For example, deep introverts and active extroverts can learn a lot from each other. A rule of thumb is that the more mature and experienced the group, the more it welcomes differences in members. The less mature and experienced, the more it resists differences. Find a balance for your group.

But do not worry too much about getting the perfect person for the perfect group. You can make the necessary changes as time reveals the nature of your group's fruit: "Likewise every good tree bears good fruit, but a bad tree bears bad fruit" (Matthew 7:17). A group where members experience grace, truth, and pain and find that life is getting better shows a different fruit from one with constant chaos, boredom, division, or alienation.

Chapter 23

Establish the Ground Rules

Small groups run better when there is enough order and structure to protect and enhance the process. Structure and ground rules refer to all the parameters a group needs. As group leader you convey, model, enforce, and inculcate that structure in the group members' lives and experiences.

We have already discussed the group frame and issues of attendance, punctuality, and consequences. We will devote more time to presenting group members' roles and responsibilities in part 5 of this book. In this chapter, however, we briefly deal with the leader's role in applying these structures to the small group.

The Ideal Is Less

How detailed should the ground rules be? Should the group monitor lateness? Ring a gong when someone interrupts? Let's start with the ideal situation, which is to *provide only the minimum amount of structure necessary to protect the group's functioning.* The fewer rules, the better—but most groups need *some* rules.

The more mature, high-functioning, and experienced the group members are, the fewer rules they need. The people make the commitment, show up on time, get involved, and respect each other's feelings. They don't require a lot of rules because they have internalized them already. That scenario illustrates Jesus' teachings about how to fulfill all the rules by following one transcendent rule: "So in everything, do to others what you would have them do to you, for this sums up the Law and the Prophets" (Matthew 7:12).

On the other hand, most groups do need a few guidelines. After establishing the frame ahead of time, you will find out what else is needed as the group begins to meet. You may need a "no interruption" ground rule or an "everyone needs to participate" ground rule. After meeting a few times with a small group of fifth-grade boys at my church, I established an "everybody keeps the chair seat connected to their bottoms, not to their knees or feet" rule. I have never had to do that in the adult groups I have led—yet. So tailor matters to whatever keeps the group going smoothly.

The Vision Is Reconciliation

Keep your structure, and how you present it to the group, in the context of why you are meeting. The group is meeting to help people reconcile their lives to God's ways in spiritual growth, parenting, dating, addictions, or whatever. Let them know that the rules are not there just to be rules, but rather to *serve the vision:* "The reason we have the ground rule of regular attendance is that people need it to feel safe and open with each other. That is how vulnerability, growth, and change occur. So if you think you may have attendance problems, maybe you and I can talk after group to see if this is the right place for you."

Accept Resistance toward You

As facilitator you are the bearer of the ground rules, the "bad news." Some group members will likely see you as a transference object. These members don't like rules, have authority conflicts, or think structure is oppressive and controlling. That is part of the cost of being a facilitator. Group members may sometimes use you to work out issues like this.

Listen to the protests, but don't take them personally. Change what is reasonable to change, but *don't remove needed structure just because it annoys someone.* You may be helping that person—and the group—learn a great deal about lovingly and gently holding to a firm value. Make it part of the group discussion: "Steve, you think that I shouldn't insist we show up on time and that I am being unreasonable. I really disagree, but let's see what others think."

Help the Group Own the Ground Rules

The group also needs to take responsibility for the structures. Give members permission to speak up to each other and hold each other accountable. Help Mary say to Brent, "I'm getting frustrated that you interrupt me and others a lot. I don't know what to do about it. Do we need to set a ground rule, like asking you to stop talking for a few minutes when we find you doing it again?"

Stay on Task

As facilitator you are also the timekeeper. If your group is to see a video, hear a lecture, or go over a study guide and then move to a more open process time, you should enforce that sequence. Move the group along even if people resist it, especially if the leaders and group experts have shown that the time plan works. People sometimes need this kind of guidance to prevent getting lost on one focus. This also helps them develop their own internal structure, which they often need. Again, if something urgent occurs, as we discussed in chapter 19 on process versus structure, be willing to be flexible so no one gets hurt.

Good facilitators and good groups are both loving and structured. Give your group both benefits in your rules and conduct.

PART 4

THE RESPONSIBILITIES OF GROUP FACILITATORS

Chapter 24

Balance Grace, Truth, and Time

As we have said many times in this book, you are not the group, nor does all that happens in the group rest on your shoulders. Remember that the more the group works as a group, the less work you do. Your job is to facilitate, to *help certain things happen.*

You're like a gardener. The gardener does not make the plants grow. She cannot control them. But she can provide the place and proper ingredient mix for the already ordained growth to occur. She can protect the plants from weeds and diseases that would impede the process and from wild animals that would destroy them. She adds water, fertilizer, pruning, latticework for weak stems, protective fencing, and plant food. Similarly, as facilitator you can help provide a proper balance of ingredients for growth and be a reminder that these ingredients come through Jesus Christ.

Maintain Balance

We have already described in detail the essential group growth ingredients of grace, truth, and time. If these ingredients are *in balance,* then growth is more likely to occur. Your job is to monitor the group's mix of the ingredients. The following tips will help you develop a mind-set to make sure that all three remain present in your group.

Remember the natural pressure toward imbalance. This pressure depends on the group makeup, the particular session, and more. Be aware of and watch for it. If, for example, a group is composed of high achievers who are hard drivers, they might naturally go toward truth. They set standards and hold themselves and each other to them, but they are poor on acceptance and helping weaknesses in each other.

Intervene when the imbalance goes on too long or is severe enough that something might be lost. Don't worry if you have a *segment of imbalance.* For example, it is okay to spend time giving truth even if that time does not have a great deal of relational feel. And remember that while the imbalance should never be something *ungraceful,* focusing only on truth for a given segment is no *more* harmful than having a meal of fruit only. But if that becomes the entire diet, then you have a problem. Figure out your group metabolism, and intervene when you see imbalance.

Different groups have different balancing quotients. A discussion group for seekers is not looking for a big download of truth, so too much truth can imbalance the group very quickly. A group of people who have been in the faith for a long time—and who really want to delve into a verse and unpack it all night—can stand more truth. In the same way, a group designed to process grief needs more times of extended grace and less input of truth. The proper balance always depends on the group purpose and makeup.

Remember the continuity of time itself. Grace and truth together for short bursts is not grace and truth together over time. All three ingredients have to be there over the long haul. Though these may be unbalanced in short bursts, guard the long haul with diligence. And remember that the imbalance is *never* something ungraceful, untruthful, or unstructured. It is just that there is more of an emphasis on one than the other.

Most important, as facilitator, **be aware of and monitor the balance.** If you don't do it, no one will, and imbalance will occur.

Offer Grace and Truth through Jesus Christ

In chapter 3 we discussed how groups that offer *either* grace *or* truth leave members wanting something different, something *more*. Your group members desperately need both, and your job is to see that they get it. The Bible says that the law was given through Moses, but grace and truth are realized through Jesus Christ (John 1:17). So you have to avoid giving them the law. Instead, have them "realize" the grace and truth of Jesus.

Plan group meetings so that members learn or experience truth in a grace-giving way. Monitor your own tone. Give truth with a sound and a stance of grace, favor, understanding, compassion, forgiveness, and acceptance. Yet, in your love, do not avoid saying the "hard thing." Remember to go "hard on the issue and soft on the person."

Guard the group process against extremes by group members. If someone is not gracious, intervene as a guardian of the process. Whatever is appropriate for your group is okay, but make sure you do it. On the one end, you might intervene in a grace-truth imbalance by saying, "Hold on, Sam. I wanted to say some things to Sue." On the other end, you might say, "Sam, that sounded harsh. Are you aware of that? Did anyone else experience that as a lack of grace?" Again, depending on what your group has decided, you can intervene at different levels. Just make sure you do not allow some members to create an imbalance.

Ask the group from time to time how they experience the balance between grace and truth. How would they like to experience it? Deeper yet, let them give feedback to each other on when and how the imbalance has occurred. Again, appropriateness is key. But even in the "non-feedback" groups you can ask how much people experience the group as safe and honest, accepting and direct.

As a leader, talk to your close friends, coaches, or mentors about how you are embodying grace and truth. Get feedback and work on it.

Remember, growth happens when all of the ingredients—grace, truth, and time—are present. As a good leader, guard the balance of grace and truth as Jesus did. Then, as you go through time with your group, growth will more likely happen.

Chapter 25

Facilitate Process

Think of a continuum that has a high school geometry lecture on the left and a walk alone in the park on the right.

What is the difference? Which one feels better to you? In which do you learn the most? Which can be done for longer periods of one's life? Which one has value?

These questions reveal issues that surface in the difference between *structured* learning—like a geometry class lecture—and *process and experience* learning, in which we observe, experience, and come to realizations through the experience. Which has value? Both do.

The trick as a small group leader is twofold. One aspect is to decide what kind of group you will have. The other is to facilitate that decision. We value both approaches but believe a mixture of structured learning and process-and-experience learning is best. If your groups turn into lecture sessions, you had better plan on a time-limited group life or have some *very* interesting information. It is tough for an "information only" group to last for years. But if you include moments of experience, realization, and process orientation—all less didactic in nature—then your group can be a valuable place of learning and growth for years.

The Power of Process-oriented Statements

A big problem is that many small group leaders have little training in how to "do process." If that sounds like an oxymoron, it sort of is. The better way to say it is "facilitate process," and that is really your job. You are to help make it happen. By its nature, process is not something that you can *do* or *control.* It *does itself.* Process is an unfolding discovery of God, ourselves, and each other in connected moments of going with the flow. It is the walk-in-the-park equivalent of group experience.

Think of how you walk in a park. Your walk has a direction. In your group, the direction is your material, content, subject matter, or structure. A divorce recovery group doesn't talk about the second coming of Christ or share recipes unless either topic somehow relates to the group purpose of helping people through the divorce process. But what if the group does wander? You might make a *process statement* about wandering off the path. This follows one of the most important rules of process: *Use what is happening in the group to get more process to happen.*

So you might *notice* the detour and say, "I notice that we were talking about how difficult it is to let go, and the subject changed to cooking. How did that happen? Why do you think that is?" As leader, you know something in this little process statement. You know that part of divorce recovery is to process the pain of divorce with others. When the pain grows too real, people sometimes change the subject. When you help the group see their tendency to avoid others' pain, they can talk about why they do that and what it means to their lives. In doing that one process statement, the group leader can:

- Get the group "back on the path" of processing their divorce pain
- Model a willingness to go deep instead of avoiding reality and life's hurts

- Show the group that there really is someone in charge and that this thing is not going to wander off into the desert but eventually make it through the park
- Get the group to experience much more connectedness as they get back on the path and get real again
- Get the group to see how they tend to avoid reality and pick certain kinds of people—and in so doing may have contributed to their divorce
- Model the way that God is with us, in that he is not afraid to seek the deeper parts of our soul
- Pave the way for healing in the group as people are held to sharing and experience love and healing from each other

All these things can come from one *process-oriented statement.* As leaders, use what you notice in the group to make it aware of what it is doing and not doing. Then the group can get back to its work of being what it needs to be for each other to do healing and growth (Ephesians 4:16).

Simple But Powerful Tips to Facilitate the Process

To be a good process facilitator you need to do things that are in themselves very simple but take time to learn. It is a big temptation for a leader just to start teaching or explaining, and sometimes that is a good thing to do. But if the group is merely a geometry class, not much bonding and healing will occur. Be aware that some of the best things in life are learned on a walk as much as in reading a book. *You can hear a lecture on trees, or you can go experience them. Life is about both.* You can read about divorce recovery, or you can experience recovery. The process group leader helps the members do both.

Notice and Share What You Observe

Notice what is going on in the group, and from time to time share what you see. Very simple, very powerful. Here are examples of how these observations may work in your group:

- "I notice that we have drifted away from the sadness. What happened?"
- "I notice that it seems a little sluggish in here tonight. Why do you think that is?"
- "It seems like we were really connecting and things changed. Why is that?" Then someone may say, "Well, I really felt judged a minute ago when I was sharing. So I just stopped." The group will often let you know what is wrong. It is a little like having an elephant in the living room, but no one is talking about it. A process question gives members an opening to discuss the matter.
- You might aim a well-timed, helpful process statement to an individual. "Joe, I notice that when you talked about that, you seemed to really be feeling some things. Can you tell us what they are?" Again, just use what is happening before your eyes, and facilitate it. In the park you look around and see a flower, and then you say, "Look! A flower. Let's go take a closer look." You don't have to create the flower; you just have to see it.
- Notice when the group is stuck and address the situation. "It feels dead in here for the past few weeks. Does anyone else notice that?" The cause might be a particular issue, such as the group's losing a member but not processing that together. Or perhaps the material or the topic has run its course and the group is ready for a change. If you do not address it, people might drop out. If you address it, the group may reinvent itself.

Be the Guardian of the Process

Do something about people who interrupt, dominate, or keep process from occurring. Different levels of intervention may be appropriate, depending on the particulars, *but do something!* You cannot allow a person to kill the group process. If the group is not oriented toward going deep on feedback, just interrupt the interrupter or over-spiritualizer. Say, "Hold on, Joe. I want to hear more from Susie." The group will feel protected by you. Joe will get the message, and the process will be saved.

Hold Members to Their Covenant

In a deeper group orientation, where members have covenanted to receive feedback, the process goes a step farther. After the initial exchange, suggested above, say to Joe, "Joe, I notice that when people talk about feelings, you often interrupt and give a Bible verse. Are you aware that you do that?" Then, if the group operates on an even deeper level, you might say, "What do some of you experience when Joe does that?" Deepest of all, when Joe interrupts, say, "Did anyone just notice what happened?" Then the group will guard the process and help Joe.

Remember, what is a suitable intervention level depends on what the group has agreed to do with each other and depends on the facilitator's skill level. It's up to you as facilitator to make sure these structures remain intact. Otherwise, deep process statements can turn into chaos or discord. *No matter what intervention level you need in order to guard the process, guard it.* Even if it just means interrupting the interrupter and saying, "Hold on. Susie was talking."

Ask Open-ended Questions

Remember that process orientation does not have to be deep or threatening. To *process* is to *experience* and to do things that further the experience. Asking open-ended questions often furthers the process:

- "What are some of your responses to the passage we just read?"
- "What is going on with some of you this week?"
- "Can you tell us more about that?"
- "Does anyone have anything they would like to share or to add?"
- "What does this bring up for you?"

- "Where do you have difficulty applying what we just read or talked about?"
- "How would some of you fill in these blanks about the passage? I think _____ about it. I feel _____ about it. I have a problem with _____ about it."

Avoid questions that do not further discovery or process, such as questions with yes or no or factual answers. Process is not a geometry class where there is a right answer. It is a walk in the park. "What stands out for you?" and "What do you see?" are questions that don't have a right or wrong answer.

Ask for Group Feedback

Ask the members from time to time how they think the process is going. "What is getting us there? What is keeping us from there?" Even more powerful at times is to see whether they can notice and describe the process. "How would some of you describe what we have been doing, what the process is? What has that been like? How would you want it to be different?"

Certainly, as we discussed in earlier chapters, teaching and information are important to your group purpose and to life. But it's just as important to *experience* that truth, particularly in relational contexts like a group. Your job as a facilitator is not to "be the experience," but to facilitate it. You are the shepherd of the experience. You are the guardian of the process. You are the gardener of the garden of experience. Whatever metaphor you like, think of it and do it. Then the group will take on a life of its own, growing in richer ways than it ever could simply through lectures.

Chapter 26

Listen

Not long ago, the small group pastor of a large church asked me (Henry) what I would suggest he do in training his small group leaders. I was surprised at how quickly I blurted, *"Teach them to listen!"* I was almost embarrassed by how forcefully I said it.

But as I thought about it, I understood why I said that. For many years I have observed facilitators so incapable of listening to others that they actually "de-facilitate" growth in the process. As I have trained group leaders over the years, it always surprises me how difficult it is to get them to listen.

A big part of the problem is that we think listening is just the ability to know what someone has said. And once we know what they have said, we feel the permission to tell them what we think or feel, or whatever we want them to listen to from us. From a facilitator's perspective, that is not listening. It is just waiting your turn.

Validate to Show You Truly Hear

Listening as a facilitator means *to hear the person and to have the person know that you have heard*. This means you have to actually say and do things that let her know she has been heard and understood, which takes a little attention and effort. The result is that a person feels validated, understood, cared for, attended to—and is better able to go further into whatever she was processing to begin with. In that way, you have facilitated something instead of de-facilitating something.

Consider some examples of the difference between de-facilitating and facilitating.

Sue says, "I guess I have just been overwhelmed this week in all that has happened. I sometimes want to give up, but then I feel like I am just having a pity party. I mean, people go through stuff like this all the time. I even feel guilty for talking about it, but it gets to me."

The leader says, "Oh, Sue. Don't be discouraged. It isn't that bad. You can do it! God can meet your needs, and we will help you get through this time. It won't be too much for you. You are a strong person."

What do you think Sue feels now? Do you think she is going to open up more to the group? Do you think she feels understood and connected with? Contrast that scenario with the next.

Sue says, "I guess I have just been overwhelmed this week in all that has happened. I sometimes want to give up, but then I feel like I am just having a pity party. I mean, people go through stuff like this all the time. I even feel guilty for talking about it, but it gets to me."

The leader responds, "Sounds like it has been *horrible* for you and then you even feel worse for feeling that way."

What do you think Sue feels now? She probably feels as if someone is really listening to her and hears what she said—and gets it. She feels connected with, and now the whole group is right there with her because the leader has met her in her reality.

I am not at all saying that it would not be appropriate at some point to encourage or build up Sue or inspire her faith in God. For example,

I could see a point in which a member might say, "Sue, we have seen that you think less of your abilities than they actually are. We have seen enormous strength and ability in you over the last months. I am really confident in your ability to figure this out and make it work."

Another member might add, "Sue, as hard as this is, I really believe that in light of all we have seen God do in the process and with all of his promises that we are learning, he is going to be there with you and strengthen you."

These and other helpful statements can build up Sue. But the key is, they come later. As Proverbs 18:13 tells us, "He who answers before listening—that is his folly and his shame." The answer is important, but only after you have really heard and understood the issue and *after the person has understood that you have understood.* The building-up statements must follow Sue's experience of knowing that the leader and others are truly with her and understand how bad things feel for her, no matter how the group sees the situation. She feels met in her reality and knows that members understand.

That kind of deep listening can bring about a reality key to what goes on in a good group: "The purposes of a man's heart are deep waters, but a man of understanding draws them out" (Proverbs 20:5).

When you truly understand a person and understand what is going on, you will draw out what is in that person instead of shutting him down. He will open up, and more of his soul will be connected to the group.

In addition to being heard, the person feels something called *validation.* Validation means that the person's *reality has been seen as real or true* for him. That does not mean you agree with his reality. It does mean you acknowledge that reality and his feelings as true for him. By contrast, *invalidation* means *negation of experience or reality.* Here are some examples of negation:

- "Oh, you don't really feel that way."
- "No, you don't really think that!"
- "Don't say that. God does love you!"

- "That isn't that bad."
- "That's not true. You are really cute!"

When you invalidate someone's experience, she tends to feel not heard and not understood. Worse, she tends to stop sharing her experience with the person or situation that invalidates her. So someone who is invalidated in your group will take her heart far away from either you or the group and then be inaccessible.

Compare the above statements with these statements of validation:

- "I can see that you feel awful about this."
- "I think I understand how you see this."
- "Sounds like you feel totally forsaken by God."
- "It feels terrible to you."
- "It feels to you like you're not attractive at all."

The first list basically says, "Your experience is not real." The second list says, "I am taking your experience very seriously and treating it with the utmost respect." This in no way says that I believe God does not love the person, only that I believe she *feels* as if God doesn't love her. And if *she* knows that I know what she feels like, we can move further down the road of processing those feelings and finding answers. But if I just negate her reality right away, I may win a debate yet lose the person.

Empathize to Show You Really Care

Empathy occurs when someone feels that you really enter into his experience and reality. This act adds immediate comfort and connection. People who receive empathy no longer feel alone. Nothing has changed in the reality of their problem or issue, but something has changed in their reality as persons: they are *no longer alone with whatever it was*. Empathy shows that you care, that you see and experience reality from the other person's point of view. Here are some tips for communicating empathy both nonverbally and verbally:

Focus on the person. Give her your eye-to-eye attention. Do not just listen while looking at your outline to figure out what is next. Show her you care by being fully present.

Give nonverbal cues, *such as nodding,* **or verbal affirmations,** *such as "Hmmm . . . oh, right . . . I see."* Use facial expressions that match what you are feeling about what she is feeling.

Use reflective statements to show that you heard. At some point include all the components she communicated, such as feelings, behaviors, and contexts. For example, Sue might say, "I don't know how to cope with three kids and no husband. It just seems like there is no end to the list of things to do. I feel like I have no life and am swamped all the time, so I find myself withdrawing. I don't like myself when I am like that and feel like a lousy mother."

The empathetic leader might reflect, "It's like there is so much required of you that you reach the end of yourself and retreat. It's too much, and then you even feel worse about yourself. That's a terrible feeling."

The leader has picked up on the feelings, the behaviors, and the experience and has also shown understanding by identifying with how terrible it is to feel that way. If you get lost, just reflect back to the person what you are hearing, in your own words. You might say, "Sounds like it is all just too much" or "It feels as if it is swallowing you up." Or you might empathize with statements such as "Doing the job of both parents by yourself feels like it is breaking you" and "I can hear that this is really hard."

Although it's important to reflect all the components you have heard, don't rush in. Give yourself time to think. A little silence after someone expresses something never hurt anyone.

Nor should you teach or rush to advise. "Why don't you call your friends to help?" does not get at the person's experience. It jumps way too far ahead.

Focus both on the content of what the person is saying as well as the feelings that go with it as you feed it back: "Your husband is not too sensitive and you begin to feel all alone." That is a basic formula that you can almost always depend on: content and feelings. Find the main idea of what someone is saying and identify how he feels about it. "Sounds like school is very demanding and you are getting discouraged."

Content + Feelings = Being Understood

In trying to empathize, listeners sometimes divert the conversation. The key is to stay focused on the speaker's content and feelings. Don't rush in and tell about what that reminds you of in your own life: "I know what that is like. When I raised my children, life was really tough."

Use statements that encourage more talking, such as "Tell me more." This shows you are listening and focused and desire to listen more. Avoid questions that divert attention from the speaker's agenda. Asking "how long has this been happening?" is a not an empathetic question when the emotion is the most important thing to hear at the moment.

Helping the person feel understood also requires that you don't change the subject, give platitudes, or judge. Avoid spiritualizing. Don't give out Bible verses when it would show greater love to just listen and understand. Sometimes "weeping with those who weep" (Romans 12:15) is a better way to live out that verse than preaching it.

Ultimately, life change happens when someone's heart is engaged in the process. If you miss his heart in the group, chances are he will miss the group and what it is trying to do as well. There will be a disconnect.

Listening makes the bridge to the heart. There is a time for answers, advice, coaching, confrontation, and teaching. But that time is always *after* someone is understood and feels understood. Feeling understood happens when the listener communicates that understanding in a usable way.

Practice your listening. And take the advice that I gave to that pastor: *Get some good listening training.* If your church does not provide such training, go to a seminar. It will help you in all of your relationships in life. For sure, it will help your effectiveness as a small group leader. You can never get too good at listening.

Chapter 27

Provide Safety

I (John) was in a group with a member who was acting out in a destructive way. Toni was taking financial steps that were jeopardizing her marriage to her husband, Ken. She reported that she had to do them to protect herself from Ken, but it was obvious to the group she was really angry and vengeful.

Toni told the group how glad she was that we were a safe place in which she could talk about these things "without getting put down or beat up." The group was quiet, and then Paul said, "Toni, I want us to be safe for you, too. And, for me, that means if I don't speak up about how hurtful you are being to your marriage, we won't be a safe place." He then clearly and lovingly told her his viewpoint on the situation. Other group members quietly agreed.

Toni blew up. She got out of her chair and said, "And I thought this was supposed to be a safe place!" She stormed out. We never saw her in group again. The members felt horrible and at first thought they had been too mean. Finally, after some time and a few meetings, they realized that they had indeed been the safest place possible for Toni. They had attended to her, graced her, heard her end of it, and gently disagreed. But Toni had chosen to walk away from safety.

Let's take a look at what safety in a small group really is and how to develop it in your setting.

More Than Comfort

The term *safety* is an important one for groups. In the Old Testament it conveys the idea of *carelessness,* that is, being so secure in a relationship that we don't have to hide or edit who we are: "I will lie down and sleep in peace, for you alone, O LORD, make me dwell in safety" (Psalm 4:8). If members are going to open up in a small group, they must know that they can be safe from injury or harm. With a safe group they can bring out thoughts, emotions, deeds, sins, hurts, and disturbing memories so the members can bring love and help for those parts of their lives.

But as in the example of Toni, safety means more than agreeing with someone and more than caring about someone. It ultimately means that the group will do whatever it takes to help the person grow. As we wrote in *Safe People,* a safe person is someone who influences you to be more of whom God intended you to be. So safety involves more than one aspect. It also involves grace, structure, time, example, and commonality.

Grace

Grace, being "for" each other as God is for us, is the foundation of safety in a small group. There is truly "no condemnation" (Romans 8:1), as each person is aware of his own need for God's love, mercy, and compassion. There is no room in grace for shame, guilt, or judgment. The group invites the hurt and dark parts of a person's soul to be connected and healed. You may want to tell the group at its beginning, "As a ground rule, we as a group are first and foremost about grace. So be aware that when one of us reveals something to the group, we need to be accepted as we are before anything else can happen."

Structure

Truth and structure also provide safety for the group. This might involve the frame, confrontation, and feedback. For example, if a person gets so emotional that he might verbally attack another member, the members know the leader will intervene. Or if people are not attending to someone in pain, the others in the group will confront that behavior as being disconnected from the person's experience. When people know there is an order and structure to the group, they are less afraid of the unpredictable, either in themselves or in others.

Time

"Carelessness" is not an immediate thing. It takes time to create, and it takes time for people to test out. Allow people time to learn it and ultimately trust the group. Tell the group, "We all want to be safe here, but we probably won't all do it right at first. So if you think someone is not being safe, bring it up and we'll all look at it until we get it right for each other."

Your Example

In your role as facilitator you not only provide teaching about safety, but also take risks yourself, so the group can see how safe the setting really is. You may want to open up about a past failure or present struggle. In addition, you can model how to be safe with someone in the group who needs attending to. For example, if someone mentions being embarrassed about a weight problem, you might say, "I am glad you took a risk about such a tough area for you. I want to know more about what it is like for you and also how other people feel toward you, now that you have opened up about it."

Commonality

The universality of experience is a powerful part of creating a safe small group. When people begin to open up, they find that others have similar struggles and that they are not alone in their suffering. This takes much of the sting out of what they are hiding. Let them know, "If you can identify with Tammy's experience, let her know, so she doesn't feel as if she's the only one who has ever felt that way."

As groups grow closer and more cohesive, they also become safer. You will be amazed at how the quality and vulnerability of what is shared changes and deepens over time as the members experience the safety and freedom from fear the group affords to them: "There is no fear in love. But perfect love drives out fear" (1 John 4:18).

Chapter 28

Clarify and Ask Questions

Sometimes one of two things happens in a group. Someone says something that people think they understand and they don't, or they know they don't and never find out. They just sit silently and wonder what the person meant by what they said. As group leader, remember that your job is active, not passive. Even when you are silent, you are actively thinking about how to facilitate the group process.

Rather than sit and wonder what someone means, get more information and seek clarity. Make sure the person and the group are connecting.

If understanding is lost, connection is lost also. And chances are that if you are somewhat confused about something, the group is also. Here are some hints on seeking clarification level by level.

The first level is **seeking the clear meaning of any ambiguity**. If someone says, "I am going to take some time off," what does that mean? What does "time" mean here—a day? a month? a year? And what does "off" mean? Leave the country? We have no idea. And even if you do, chances are that others in the group do not. So just ask. "What do you mean 'time off'?" or "What does that look like?"

Deeper levels of clarification add to the awareness of the person himself. **Asking questions about an emotional issue** helps the person actually find out more. If he says, "I have been feeling rejected lately," for example, that leaves a lot of room for the person and the group to discover more. You might ask, "What kind of feeling is that?" or "What do you mean by 'rejection'?" That could easily lead the person to answer, "Well, maybe rejection is the wrong word. I guess it is more that my wife disapproves of some things, and I take it as rejection." In response to the "feeling" question, the person might say, "It is an old feeling that I recognize from most of my life. I think it began when my parents divorced when I was a teenager." The point is that we never know where seeking clarification will go. That is one of the great things about seeking more. It leads us to more of the person and also leads the person to more of himself. And it allows the members to know each other better and provide more for each other.

Use the group as a thermometer to see how clear something is. Ask them at times if they know what a member meant to say. "Was that clear to you guys?" "Did everyone understand what he meant by that?"

At other times you can ask directly for clarification on things you wonder about. You could wonder and ask, "What all went into that decision to take so much time off?" Your question would clarify it for you and the group. It would also give the person a chance to talk more about the whole issue.

Seek clarification when someone gives conflicting data. "You said you really want to go out with this person, and you also said he 'scares' you. Can you explain that contradiction?" Ask for specificity. "What specifically do you mean when you say that she is 'abusive'?"

Hold the person to the exact meaning if she seems to say one thing but imply another. "Is this what you are really saying? That if we don't agree with your decision to leave your husband, we don't care about you? Is that what you are really thinking here?"

Seek out the thinking behind what people say. "How do you think that is going to help? How would leaving solve things?" Get to what has gone on in their heads behind a decision. Clarify what is behind a feeling. "What exactly is making you feel that way?"

Sometimes repeating the person's words leads to more information. "You said the relationship started to go bad when he was unfaithful." A statement like that invites the person to offer more information.

If you feel lost in the mire, just say so. "I am getting a little lost here. What are you trying to say?" This will get the person to focus better.

If there are gaps in the information, ask about them. "I think you might have skipped some things. We don't know how you got to where you are. Bring us up to speed."

Remember the different aspects of listening—feelings and content—as a map for what you are trying to draw out. "Is it the whole relationship or his unfaithfulness that has gotten to you?" "What do you end up feeling about it?"

Remember that if you as facilitator need to know more or don't understand something, the other members probably feel the same way. Protect your group and its process. Be an advocate for it. If the group is suffering or in the dark, intervene. The members will be happy that you did.

Chapter 29

Confront

Webster defines *confront* in two ways. See which one comes to mind for you:

1 : to face especially in challenge : **OPPOSE 2 a** : to cause to meet : bring face-to-face <*confront* a reader with statistics> **b** : to meet face-to-face : **ENCOUNTER** <*confronted* the possibility of failure>

Most of us think of confronting in the adversarial way, bringing up all sorts of scary images and feelings. It is rare that we think of it simply as meeting something face to face.

To confront can mean that we just encounter something—about ourselves, others, or reality itself. Confrontation does not have to be adversarial at all. Actually, it is one of the most loving things we can do for each other. To confront literally means to *face* something. It means to *look at* something, to *turn your face toward and look at it frontally.* In other words, all it means is that we are going to *stop avoiding seeing* something that is true. What could be more loving than helping someone to see what is true?

That is exactly what happens in the best groups. People lovingly help each other see things that are true. True about themselves, others, God, life, and all things that groups focus on. A well-functioning group helps its members to get more in touch with reality on all those fronts.

Barriers to Confrontation

The problem is that people face many barriers regarding confrontation:

- They have had bad experiences, perhaps while growing up, of confrontation as mean or harsh.
- They have critical aspects of themselves that make any feedback sound harsh once it gets inside their head.
- They lack good experiences in confrontation, so they don't expect good things to happen.
- They do not have the skills to do it themselves and therefore fear the whole topic.
- Being confronted forces them to look at things that may be frightening or painful.
- They carry a lot of guilt.
- They are embarrassed.

But, as we said earlier, finding out things we did not know about ourselves is one of the most helpful things that can happen to us. Also, in areas we know about but are not facing, we need help. If we are in denial about something destructive in our lives, we need a little help to take ownership. The Bible is full of passages that tell us to do that for each other. It is a little like having an alarm system to tell us that the house is on fire and we must do something about it.

Modes of Confrontation

A good group uses different confrontation modes, and each is important. The leader confronts members. The leader sees something and brings it to the member's attention for him and the group to deal with: "Joe, it seems that you are ignoring the seriousness of this problem. You kind of laugh it off, but it is really hurting your family."

Sometimes the leader confronts the whole group: "I notice that the group has not been opening up tonight as you usually do."

Confrontation between members—probably the most powerful mode—results from good facilitation. Remember, it is always better when the group is doing the work rather than the leader. The leader facilitates and the group does the work. Someone causes an individual or the group itself to encounter something they have not seen or avoid dealing with. Confrontation makes them aware and brings them to a point of dealing with that awareness.

Your job as leader is to make sure that appropriate confrontation occurs, in keeping with the kind of group you have established. Whether you confront the issue yourself or facilitate it, it has to happen. Groups confront many things that members may not be seeing or dealing with:

- Feelings
- Attitudes
- Behaviors and choices
- Thinking and beliefs
- Talents, strengths, and gifts
- Values
- Desires
- Denial
- Patterns
- Discrepancies between words and emotions, or words and actions
- Relationships
- Spiritual patterns and realities
- Communication styles
- Parenting
- Lack of love, judgmentalism, control, detachment, haughtiness

- Dating patterns
- Discrepancies between stated goals and actual behavior in the group
- Self-defeating patterns and attitudes
- Distortions of self and others
- Lack of ownership
- Minimizing
- Inappropriate dependency
- Blaming
- Discrepancies between group behavior and outside world behavior
- Mistrust
- Failures
- Self-perceptions
- Passivity
- Addictions

Tips for Good Confrontation

As Proverbs 27:5 tells us, "Better is open rebuke than hidden love." Confrontation is a gift, sometimes even a lifesaving gift. But it has to be done well.

Prepare for Confrontation

Talk to the group to prepare and orient them about the level and ways they would like to hear confrontation from each other. Take their temperature about it. What have been their experiences?

Have some time for each person to tell how he prefers to be confronted and how he may react to group feedback. Get on the same page as far as expectations, appropriateness of the members, and appropriateness of the group for giving feedback.

Remember the axiom "Soft on the person, hard on the issue." Make that a ground rule, if necessary.

Start with Affirmation and Empathy

Start with affirmation. "Joe, I like you and appreciate you. Because of that, there is something I think you need to know that might help you." Express empathy for the problem that you are confronting. "And I feel for you in this situation. It seems so difficult."

"Notice" Works Better Than "Should"

State your thoughts as opinions or observations instead of "you should" instructions. "Joe, I have noticed that sometimes your work and other things seem to leave no room for your family. The way you describe your life sounds to me like there is not much room for them." That is a lot better than "You should stop working and be at home!"

Other helpful ways to begin confrontations include:

- "I notice that. . . ."
- "I have seen that you. . . ."
- "Have you noticed that . . . ?"
- "Are you aware of the fact that . . . ?"
- "One of the things I have seen you do. . . ."
- "I think that. . . ."
- "The way that I experience you is. . . ."
- "I experience what you are saying differently than you do [good or bad]. . . ."
- "I wonder if you have ever thought about how you. . . ."

Combine Grace and Truth

Remember to have grace with your truth. Remember that the group looks at you as a model. So, with everything you say, combine grace and truth, love and honesty, caring and directness to show members how confrontation is done.

Try to get the group to do the confrontation, modeling that same helpful combination. "What do some of you think about what is going on with Joe?"

Is Feedback Desired?

Ask the one who needs to be made aware of something if he would like to hear some feedback. "Joe, would you like some feedback from me and the group about our thoughts on this?"

Be Specific

Be clear on what the issue is. Don't beat around the bush. As Paul says, by "speaking the truth in love, we will in all things grow up ..." (Ephesians 4:15). That's why we have to come clean with each other: "Therefore each of you must put off falsehood and speak truthfully to his neighbor, for we are all members of one body" (Ephesians 4:25). Point out discrepancies, distortions, defensiveness, games, and smoke-screens in the process of confrontation.

Describe the different aspects of what you see, including feelings and behaviors. Often it is helpful, at least in the beginning, to give concrete examples of what you are talking about and have noticed. "I have heard you say that you broke up with six different women in the last two years. I would think that that reveals some sort of problem, don't you?"

Confront Because You Care

Keep in mind that sometimes the group is the only thing standing between a person and total self-destruction. Don't be afraid to save someone's life (Galatians 6:1).

Always identify with others as equal, mutual, imperfect people. Keep the attitude of "we are all trying to figure it out," and do not lord over others.

Keep in your mind, and in the group's mind, the definition of *confront* as *encountering* things. Confrontation does not always have to be adversarial; it can be a way for us to help each other see and encounter the truth about ourselves.

Again, all of this presupposes that you have the kind of group that is prepared for feedback and finds confrontation appropriate. If that is true, then, when done correctly and lovingly, telling each other the truth can be one of the greatest gifts the group can give to itself.

Chapter 30

Set Limits

As a small group leader, you are like the gardener trying to facilitate growth and fruitfulness. You want certain things to happen or occur. You are looking for *more* of something. It is about increase.

The negative side of producing increase has to do with getting rid of the things that prevent or damage the growth process. A gardener has a fence to keep out animals that would destroy the garden. He walks through the garden on a regular basis, getting rid of weeds that would choke growth.

In the same way, a facilitator has to put up fences against things that would hurt the group process or an individual. She has to set limits on behavior, attitudes, communication, and other things destructive to individuals or the group. Also, the leader facilitates the group's setting its own limits. You can do that by making process statements or just checking in with the group when an issue arises and having them talk about it.

In any case, or however you do it, you must see the importance of setting limits on destructive things if your garden is going to grow. If you are too passive and let bad things go on for too long, the group will deteriorate.

Enforce Ground Rules

When you have set the ground rules for the group, make sure that you enforce them. If you don't, they are not really rules. Remember that there are many levels of setting limits. All a limit means is that you are restraining something from occurring or continuing to occur. If your group has a ground rule against interrupting each other, you have a wide range of choices on how to enforce that rule:

- *Signals*—such as raising a hand to indicate that an interrupter should wait until the speaker has finished.
- *Indirect statement about the issue*—"Group, let's make sure we let each other finish talking."
- *Direct statement*—"Joe, let her finish."
- *Direct statement about the issue that has occurred*—"Joe, are you aware that you interrupt a lot? I need for you to let people finish."
- *Direct statement to the group*—"Are you guys aware of the interrupting that goes on? Would you like to talk about it to each other?"
- *Indirect statement to the group*—"Is anyone noticing anything that just happened?"
- *Out of group, direct statement*—"Joe, I did not want to mention this in front of the group, but there is something I want to talk to you about that I think is interfering with the group process."
- *Out of group, indirect*—Change the meeting time and don't call Joe. (I'm just kidding, but probably all group leaders can identify with this desire!)
- *Consequences*—Talk to the group about an issue, like tardiness or absenteeism, and decide that if someone is late a third

time, they can't come in and interrupt, or that someone is out of the group after missing a certain number of sessions. Of course, all of that is written down and is totally the prerogative of the group. For example, some people's work schedule does not allow attendance at all meetings. Or some groups do not even work that way, like recovery groups. But the point here is that if there is a *problem* in terms of what everyone has decided, then it can be addressed and limited with consequences.

- *Appeal to higher authorities*—Sometimes the infractions are such that you must involve higher authorities, such as a program director, overseeing pastor, or even the police, to set the limits.

Choose Limits That Protect

The limits you set totally depend on what you have decided you do not want. Obviously, you will limit whatever harms the group's basic process, function, design, or purpose. For example, cross-talk is desired in some groups and not in others. (See chapter 39.) If you don't want cross-talk in your group, but it occurs anyway, then set limits on it.

Remember to set limits that are protective *and* redemptive. You want to protect the group yet help people learn from the experience. Members will experience your limits as redemptive if you put grace and truth together and go hard on the issue but soft on the person.

Define Consequences and Reconciliation

When you set limits, figure out when and if consequences are in order, and how someone can make it right with the group. Always reconcile, if possible. It's often appropriate to set limits outside the group, especially if the group is not one where everyone has agreed to deeper processing or confrontation. You may need to talk to a member—outside of a session—about her behavior and its group effects. Get some agreement on resolution and a plan.

Sometimes we set individual limits that are mostly for the good of the individual. Other times the behavior is hurting the group. Either way, confront self-destructiveness. It is the responsibility of the body of Christ to help each other by limiting the destructiveness of sin in our lives (Matthew 18:15–20).

Decide with the group what limits you all want, though remember that some limits are not optional. For example, if your group includes someone with a serious problem like substance abuse, limits are in order, especially if the problem occurs during the group time. It is possible that the group is the only thing between the self-destructive person and serious life consequences.

Last, remember that you are preserving what is valuable and good. Limits are a part of life. Whether stopping a spiritualizer or deciding that someone is not appropriate for the group and will be asked to leave, you are doing something good. You are protecting something valuable, even if it involves some pain.

Setting limits can be a hard thing. It makes both the facilitator and the group uncomfortable at times. But for good things to flourish, we have to limit the weeds. As a facilitator, that is part of your job. Take a deep breath, get some coaching, and good luck.

Chapter 31

Be an Authority

There was a key difference between the way Jesus facilitated growth and the way the Pharisees stunted it. He was *authoritative,* and they were *authoritarian.* In other words, Jesus displayed power from the strength of his truth, not the strength of pressuring people and lording himself over them. The authority came from his powerful word, not from taking a superior stance.

In fact, the Bible tells us that Jesus avoided that stance (Philippians 2:3, 5–7). He spoke the truth so powerfully that he impressed people more than did the Pharisees, who put themselves above others and talked down to them (Matthew 23:4, 13). Paul says we are to consider each other "better" than ourselves. Let the power of what you say come from your words, not from the stance of talking "over people."

Do this by watching your attitude and your language. Try to take the attitude of coming "alongside of the group," as opposed to being the teacher "over the group." In your language, watch for parental sayings such as *should* and *ought*. Use as many *I* statements as you can from a sharing perspective instead of an imperative perspective. "I think you would benefit from . . ." instead of "You should get your act together." Even strong statements are better in the *I* format: "I think that if you don't get your act together, you are going to be in real trouble." That is powerful, but not parental.

People change when they are free to make a choice. Parental stances, which lord power over people, turn them into children who will seek an adolescent rebellion in order to establish their freedom. Don't become another parent whom they will have to separate from or resist or rebel against. Become another adult who has powerful things to say. *Authority* means, among other things, "expert." Be an expert—at least in communicating equality—and the hearer will be free to choose a better way. In short, don't talk down to people or treat them like children. You are not there to baby-sit, but to facilitate adults' making better choices for their lives. Preserve their equality as adults and their freedom to not do what you say or think, and they will be more likely to respond to your truth.

Chapter 32

Require Integration

One of the group's most miraculous functions is how it helps people integrate. Briefly defined, *integration* is the capacity to experience all of our parts and feelings with another person's parts and feelings. God's light of healing touches all aspects of an integrated person's soul. There is no hiding. Each part grows in grace and truth, operating in harmony with each other part: "For you were once darkness, but now you are light in the Lord. Live as children of light" (Ephesians 5:8–9).

When a person is not integrated, he experiences division, splitting, and conflict within himself and his relationships. He cannot be all of himself. Like the man who both asks and doubts God at the same time, "he is a double-minded man, unstable in all he does" (James 1:8). He will often have one way of being one day and another the next. Or he will have a secret life that causes him great turmoil. Or he will ultimately have tendencies and relational patterns that hurt his life. Here is how the group leader can promote integration in its members.

Present It as a Group Requirement

Show the group that this is how growth and healing work. Tell them, "The group will help you meet your goals for growth and healing the more you allow yourself to be fully known and get to know others. As we bring all parts of ourselves into the group, we bring the elements of grace and truth to bear on us. It may not be pleasant, but it will really help."

Provide Grace for All Parts

One reason people stay divided and do not integrate themselves is that they fear the group will accept only their "good" parts, but condemn or withdraw from their "bad" parts. When a person brings out a shameful or vulnerable aspect of herself, say things like, "Cindy, it must be hard for you to bring up how helpless you feel about your son's drug problem. It makes me feel closer to you, just that you brought this issue up. Can anyone else let Cindy know how they feel toward this part of her life?"

Help People Lead with Weakness, Not Strength

Develop a culture and an expectation in your group that weakness and brokenness are why they are there. Each member is working on integrating into their lives the weakness and brokenness they have denied. Strength, success, and joy are important to share and must not be devalued, but you don't go to physical therapy and work out the knee that is not twisted. Say, "It seems like we are all talking about how well we are doing. I wonder if anyone is anxious about bringing up problems or struggles tonight?"

Become Aware of Missed Parts and Emotions

When a person is not integrated, there will be a lack in his life. For example, he may not be able to be direct and emotionally connected at the same time. Or he may not be able to feel sad feelings, only positive ones. Train members to become more self-aware by saying things like, "Becky, you are really good about supporting other people's issues, but it seems that we never really get around to you. I know that you're here for a reason. What is going on with you today?"

Confront the Victim-Persecutory Stance

One common problem the group can help integrate is the tendency to see oneself as a victim—and therefore exempt from being confronted. A person with this issue will present a problem or struggle to the group and ask for support and comfort. When the group goes further than that and addresses how he contributes to his situation, the person then experiences the group as dangerous and persecutory. The group's grace has little effect on him.

Help the group to love and accept that person, but also make him aware of this tendency, and its cost: *it not only distances him from them, but it keeps him unable to grow or solve his problems.* For example, "Dave, when Martha mentioned that you seemed to blame all your unhappiness on your wife's lack of support, she sounded caring and on target to me. Yet you became really hurt and angry with her. It seems that when we give you feedback, you see us as not understanding or caring about you. Can we work on this as an issue?" This can be highly valuable material. It helps people who have been stuck in a helpless mode to work out of it and integrate their power, ownership, and responsibility into the rest of their lives.

A group that requires integration helps its members be aware of, face, confess, and bring into healing the parts of themselves that may have kept them in life problems for many years. Its value cannot be overestimated.

Chapter 33

Allow Silent Moments

People new to a group process often are afraid of silence. It makes them uncomfortable and they don't see value in it. As leader you must train the group that the reality is just the opposite: *silence is part of the group process and has value in and of itself.* Silence is not a parenthesis between periods of growth; it brings growth, just as talking does. There is "a time to be silent and a time to speak" (Ecclesiastes 3:7), and the good leader can tell the difference.

The Value of Silence

When the group encounters moments of quiet, the lack of noise allows good things to happen. Silence can be a context for several processes.

Reflection and pondering. Members can think about something that just happened in group and what it means for them. More than just gaining information, people gain insight about what they are experiencing.

Internal awareness. People use silence to get in touch with what is going on inside them; they can shed the adaptive selves that life requires them to wear and experience what is truly there.

Group awareness. Members learn to sense what is going on in the room with other people. Is someone hurt or in need? Angry? Is there conflict in the room? Does someone show signs of detachment?

Serendipity. Some group silences have to do with a sense of well-being or joy because something really good just happened in the process. For example, a member was able to discuss a painful topic she had never told anyone about, and the group did a good job of being there with her. People may lapse into silence just to enjoy what God did in the room with her and with them.

Next moves. The group can use silence to make sense of whatever has been happening and develop conclusions, insights, applications, and directions for growth in their lives. They might use the silence to decide what they want to say next in the group.

Addressing Problems with Silence

Of course, there is a balance in a good group between good discussion and good silence. The facilitator needs to develop the skill for discerning when silence, or the lack of it, is a problem.

Starting off group. Typically, the most silent time in a group is likely to occur at the beginning. There are valid reasons for this, as people have come in from their outer lives or are transitioning into the group setting or may be preoccupied with something that has captured their attention elsewhere. So allow a little settling in silence at the beginning. In fact, if your group structure allows it, start off with silence rather than with a question or thought. This increases the chances that what might be most important will surface.

Transition points. When some topic has been resolved, or a person is done working on a matter for now, let the group quiet down a bit. Allow them to pay attention to whatever is going on so they can choose the next direction to go. Avoid the facilitator's temptation of saying, "Okay, who has something else to share now?" That tends to disrupt the previous matter's resolution. Moreover, it hooks those people-pleasing members who want to help you be happy that you are a good leader!

Anxiety about silence. You may find some members have a pattern of rescuing the group, and themselves, from silence. They get chatty or try to draw someone out to fill up the space. Inquire about this: "Jill, it seems as though when we all get quiet, you come up with something to discuss. Tell us what it is like for you inside when no one is talking." You may find, for example, that Jill is afraid of strong emotions—hers or anyone's—and interprets silence as a sign that a bad storm is brewing. So she diverts the "buildup" with chatting. She may need to be reassured that if feelings come up, the group can handle them.

The unstated statement. Sometimes silence means people are feeling or experiencing something but are afraid to say it. That is, *the silence itself is saying something.* As a leader you can deal with this by saying something on the order of "When Joe came in late again, you all got quiet, but several of you seem annoyed or angry. Is there something going on here with your feelings toward Joe?" Obviously, you need to be careful not to interpret silence your way, but toward what is really going on.

We live in a noisy world, yet God speaks to us in our silence. Help develop your group into a place where they create silence to hear themselves, others, and God.

Chapter 34

Interpret Themes, Symbols, and Meanings

Proverbs 20:5 says that the "purposes of a man's heart are deep waters, but a man of understanding draws them out." We are deep, complex creatures, and the Bible says in many ways that we do not always understand what is going on with us. We cannot see the forest for the trees. We can't always understand our behavior or even our own thoughts. David prayed for God to "try me, and know my anxious thoughts" and "see if there be any hurtful way in me" (Psalm 139:23–24 NASB). We need help to understand ourselves and our lives.

Often the message of our lives is hidden in symbols, symbolic behavior, or metaphors. A group member had a series of relationships in which the men left her. She could not see past the pain of the last one to the bigger message in these relationships. But the group helped her see it. "It seems," someone said, "that you only attach to men that are abandoners. Maybe being abandoned by men is more that just about Joe or Tom. Maybe it has to do with the larger story of your life. It seems that the abandoning man is a central character in your story. It would be good to find out what that means." She ended up seeing that she was repeating a pattern that had begun with an alcoholic father in childhood. But until someone pointed it out to her, she had not seen the issue: abandoning men. She had only seen the immediate problem, which she thought was Joe or Tom.

Another example was a group where a woman was talking about feeling low and somewhat depressed. When she was asked about her last year, she related it in a simple biographical way, reporting a lot of incidents. The incidents included a move, a daughter's graduation, a parent's death, and a promotion. But the leader recognized that they all added up to a theme: "It looks like you have had many things happen this year that have added up to a lot of loss. Even good things, like your daughter graduating, your promotion, and the move, involve losing people or losing contact with them. Maybe that is why you are depressed."

Recently a woman called us on our radio program and said she had been feeling abandoned in many relationships. When we asked her about them, she described, one by one, relationships with men in which something—always bad—had happened that led her to decide the relationship was not for her. In other words, she had left the relationships. Yet she was describing herself as "abandoned."

We pointed out the theme. "You say you are feeling abandoned, yet you are doing the leaving. What is it about staying that frightens you? What is it about being the one who leaves that is difficult for you to see? Why do you think you leave so much?" Now, because she saw a theme she had never recognized, she had something to work on. Sometimes we unknowingly live out themes and patterns, but once they are seen, we can resolve them and subsequently see them coming. As long as unresolved things are in our heart, they will create "issues" in our lives (Proverbs 4:23 KJV).

In addition to themes and symbols, we sometimes hint in communication about what needs to be brought out in the open. We might merely show it by our expression or leak it in a hidden word, but it is there, and the skilled leader picks up on it for the group to see and work with. "You say you are looking forward to seeing your family, but I don't really hear a lot of excitement." Often the person is not aware of the hidden feeling or implied attitude, or he is aware but afraid to say it directly. When the leader interprets or draws it out, it is in the light and more likely to be owned.

Our real meanings and issues are hidden from us in many ways. Until they become manifest, it is often difficult to resolve them. A group can help resolve hidden issues if it remembers these guidelines:

Connect the dots with what a person is saying, and present them as one solid line. For the woman we described above, one year of events added up to the theme of loss. Just listen for the theme, then make the theme manifest. In that way the theme becomes the issue.

Watch for meanings in the person's behavior. "You say you want a significant relationship, but you only ask out women who for some reason will not be available for that. Your behavior must mean you are at odds with what you say you want, or you would be asking out women who are truly eligible and would qualify."

Watch for the symbols in people's behavior as well. "It seems that all the spare-time activities you pick involve aggression. You have told us about paint-ball shooting, watching war movies and action movies, watching old reruns of fights, going shooting a lot lately. Do you think you are feeling angry about something? Or does all this express some other aggressive feelings?"

As Jesus said, careless words have meaning (Matthew 12:36). *Watch for them.* They often imply a lot about a person. Spotlighting those words can be enlightening. "Sam, did you know that each time you speak of church you say something sarcastic, in a joking way? I wonder if that is really just joking or if you are feeling more than that." Or, "Susie, are you aware of how many sexual comments you make? They are funny to be sure, but what do you think that is about?"

Interpretation is much more enigmatic, but helpful as well. It is enigmatic because you do not know if your interpretation is right or wrong. In drawing out themes and connections, things are still open to interpretation. We may not know what something means; we just know it is there. In proposing an interpretation you are venturing to say what you think something actually means to someone. Take the example of the man who dates ineligible women. To interpret it would mean that you add, "And I wonder if you are not picking eligible women because you are afraid that they will leave you like your wife did." With interpretations, it is usually best to frame them as questions or "wonderings." After all, you don't know, and that gives space for the person to consider things.

Make sure it is *appropriate,* according to group agreement, for you to connect and interpret meanings. If it is not, then you can usually do some sort of interpreting of the group as a whole, like a process view of the entire group's theme. "It seems that the group has a theme. We start looking at a page of Scripture and then end up talking about our lives." That can take them to a deeper experience of what they are doing. But to interpret things for an individual puts people more on the spot. Make sure that your action is part of the group rules and purposes and that the people are appropriate for it.

Socrates said the unexamined life is not worth living. We would add it is difficult to live very well at all without continuing examination— by God, others, and ourselves. A group is a great place for us to examine our lives, and a great tool for examination is drawing out meanings from our behavior, communications, and choices. Listen a little more deeply, and connect dots for people. As you do, the group will learn how to do it as well. With that kind of examination, we think you will also find deeper meaning.

Chapter 35

Help Contain Strong Emotions

I f you have any experience with group process, you are aware that it is a very meaningful time, but can also be tumultuous. People come with life problems, inner fragilities, and wounds, and God's design is for the body to help handle and heal them.

Therefore it is wise to have an approach for dealing with emotional crises. We use the term *emotional* because a person may have a life crisis (medical emergency, family issue, financial loss) and still be pretty stable emotionally, drawing on internal resources, God, and group support. An emotional crisis occurs when a person cannot manage, experience, and resolve feelings, with the result that the feelings either get too intense or escalate and interfere with normal life functioning.

Life crises aside, an emotional crisis can be triggered by something happening in the group. For example, because of the safety of the group, someone might start experiencing old unresolved feelings and memories she might not have been aware of. This can be very disruptive and frightening for her. If the group has little experience with being with someone in distress, it will look to you for help and guidance.

Basically, the group helps members in emotional crisis by *containment*, briefly defined as *absorbing and tolerating that which the member cannot bear alone*. When people are so injured and broken that they cannot handle strong emotions, or when the emotions are catastrophic, they may need a place to "place" the feelings so that the intensity can be shared and soothed.

Researchers have observed mothers' containing functions with infants. The baby becomes panicky, enraged, or distressed. The baby's cries escalate, as the emotions grow too large for him. The mother holds him, allows him to feel his feelings, provides a safe and structured environment for him (her arms), and absorbs his troublesome emotions into herself. In time he calms down and becomes stable. That is similar to how a group operates in crisis. Here are some tips:

Have an approach for what must be referred out. The group cannot handle every crisis. Leaders need training in recognizing when a crisis should be referred out. For example, if a person becomes suicidal, cannot resolve the crisis over time, becomes less able to function in life, or becomes a danger to other people, you will need to make some referral to appropriate resources. If your church or organization does not provide such help, find a therapeutic setting that does. You will learn to recognize important warning signs.

Be present. Help your members to be emotionally present for the person in crisis, like the mother with the baby. It is amazing how much good this does for the person in distress. Sometimes "being there" is enough to help the member internalize grace and stability so he can come out of the stormy feelings. Help the group learn to operate this way: "Bill, we're here and we are available. Keep talking about it. It's okay." Over time, you will notice the person coming out of the crisis and becoming more soothed and calm.

Help with catastrophic thinking. The person in crisis often fears that things are worse than they really are, and this escalates emotions even more. After you have helped the person to connect and confess her deep and intense emotions, use the group to help her sort out what is real and what is not. Say, "Now that you seem more comforted, let's talk about some realities. Your husband told you he is disappointed in the marriage, and you interpreted that as the end of the world. Perhaps instead, it just means that he sees some problems and wants to work on them. I think you may need more information before you conclude it's as scary as your feelings are telling you."

Develop a plan. Help the member form a practical plan to deal with the issue. A person in crisis feels helpless to do anything about the situation. When you help him take some steps, the steps provide a structure and the helplessness lessens. For example, a member with a teen on drugs might have a plan to call an adolescent specialist or even the police if necessary.

Keep a structure. While giving good attention and presence to the person, try as much as possible to keep the group structure intact. That may mean saying, "Sharon, you seem better now, after the group went through your fear with you. Are you ready now for us to move on to someone else?" This is not being cold. Rather, it conveys to the members that feelings are not always reality and that people can have strong emotions, confess and resolve them, and go on in life. It takes the unrealistic power away from intense emotions and gives people power over them to make their own choices.

Groups and emotions often go together. Be sure that as a leader you are aware of your own emotions as well as any fears of being around people who feel things deeply. Make sure you have a place in life where you also can be contained when you need it.

PART 5

THE RESPONSIBILITIES
OF GROUP MEMBERS

Chapter 36

Expect the Unexpected

Spiritual growth and group experiences are full of surprises. When dealing with God, we never really know what will happen next. While getting to know people at a deeper level, we don't really know what to expect, either. Both processes lead us to greater knowledge and experience of ourselves, including our fears, and have unexpected breakthroughs. All in all, the spiritual growth experience with God and others in a group is an adventure that just can't be predicted.

Cast the Vision

We hope your group members will catch this same spirit of adventure. We think it's their role and responsibility to ask for the unexpected and develop a mind-set of openness to whatever God wants to do in their lives through the group. Members in a good, growing group accept responsibility to give up rigid patterns of interacting, discarding old "wineskins" of spiritual interaction with others.

Members show their stance of openness to whatever God wants to do, through asking questions like these:

- "What does God have for me tonight?"
- "What does God have for me in the next year in this group?"
- "How does God want to use this person in my life?"
- "I have never seen or experienced this before. What can I learn?"

Members give up control and fixed expectations of the group experience. They allow God and the process to take them places they have never been in order to be stretched and to grow. Group members with an open attitude will grow the most. They'll also find this kind of flexibility good for life in general.

Your job, then, is to help the group to catch this vision of being open to God's unexpected work.

Air Expectations

In preparation, talk with members about their expectations of the group. Acknowledge expectations for hope, growth, and learning as predictors of a good group experience. Explain that another predictor for a good group experience is the expectation for surprise, for giving up rigidity and being stretched. Ask the group how open they are to being surprised by God. Talk about it directly as a concept related to humility and growth. Discuss how being humble before God puts us in a stance where he can grow us in unexpected directions and areas. To be humble before him is to not know what he is going to do, nor even to know what we need. To be humble is to be the clay and realize that he is the potter. It means being flexible and pliable before him.

Ease Fears

Ask members to voice their fears about being surprised by experiences to come. What are they afraid of? Are some areas off limits? What are their feelings about being open to new things happening?

You might ease their fears by suggesting that you covenant with each other to encourage one another to be open to new things and stretching experiences.

Model Openness

Remember, openness is not something you can easily dictate, but is more of a cultural thing within a group. You set the stage by continually casting a vision, starting with your opening prayer each week: "God, please help us be open to whatever you want to show us tonight."

Look for ways to sell the idea of being open to new insights, ways of being, and ways of seeing God, themselves, and life. The concept is more caught than taught, but both means are important. Finally, members can't be open if you are not. So start with yourself. You might say, "Okay, group. I want to learn something about me that I have never seen and grow in ways I have not expected. When you see how I need to grow, let me know! I want the unexpected from you."

Go before God and others and see how open you are to expecting the unexpected. Don't be the ceiling of the group, but the sunroof to the heavens.

Chapter 37

Be Known

It is a common scenario in our lives as psychologists. Someone comes for help because her marriage is in trouble or she's seriously depressed or addicted. Or the problem might be infidelity or significant problems with a child. Things have reached the level of the "last straw," so she has come to see a professional. Often people don't come to us until they've experienced significant pain for quite a while. They are just now seeking help. In other words, they have waited much past the point when they actually needed it.

As we find out more about their lives, we always want to know about their level and extent of support. We ask, "Who knows about the problem? Who has been helping? Who do you lean on and share with? Who gives you input and wisdom?"

Sometimes the client will say, "Well, I go to church" or "I have friends I am close to." Then we push a bit and ask, "But are you processing all of this with them, telling them how bad it is, and letting them really get in?" And the answer is, "No. I haven't told them what I have told you."

That is sad for us. Yet it is common for people to see church as a place where you go once a week to hear a sermon, say hi to friends, and smile at everyone. In their friendships they often share strong bonds of care and love, but the extent to which they are known is very shallow. There is sort of an "uninformed care" between them. In light of this common scenario, we must educate people on their need for more than "shallow church" or "shallow friendship." We teach them about going deeper with some people, both in a community of faith and in individual friendships. Then, as they learn the principles of being known, they improve and life begins to get on the right track.

Remaining Unknown in a Group

We also see a scenario sadder than that one. *The person is not really known, yet he is in a small group.* He comes to therapy when life is breaking down, and we ask, "Who knows about all this pain, struggle, or temptation?" And the answer is, "No one." At that point we want to scream, "What about your support group? What about your accountability group?"

Of course, people give reasons, but that is no excuse. The small group should have been a place where the person was getting at least the support of being known, held up, and understood, if not a lot more. So, in our way of thinking, there are two problems to be solved. The first problem is whatever is wrong in the person's life (such as depression or a marriage problem); the second is whatever is wrong in the person's group.

Often the group itself is not a safe place or does not have good facilitation. But sometimes the person himself is not fulfilling his role of being known. It's your job as facilitator to help the members accomplish this.

Acknowledge Resistance

Educate members well from the start that being known is a high group value. In your orientation, let people know that being known is part of their role as a group member and is important to the group's developing its values and culture and fulfilling its goals.

You will also want to educate them about the problem of resistance. The Bible plainly teaches that humans have a problem: we hide our true selves. Adam and Eve sinned and "then the eyes of both of them were opened, and they realized they were naked; so they sewed fig leaves together and made coverings for themselves" (Genesis 3:7).

Ever since then, we have continued to hide our most vulnerable selves. But while we expect this resistance, the Bible also tells us to stop hiding. Coming clean is necessary for a deep group experience. "Therefore each of you must put off falsehood and speak truthfully to his neighbor, for we are all members of one body" (Ephesians 4:25).

Let members know that there is a human force at work in the group to hide who they are, and there is a spiritual force by God to get them to stop hiding and be honest. Make this a common understanding so it becomes part of the culture.

Help to Stop Hiding

Have the group share what some of their fears are of being known. Tell them we all fear sharing our inner selves because we might experience judgment, rejection, shame, shoulds, or even intimacy. See if members can talk about what keeps them hiding. In the very act of sharing what they are afraid of, they are starting to share and thus are getting better.

Ask the group what helps them to stop hiding and how other members can help. This request will have practical results in that the group will know what to do for the person. Things will go better when they do share. Also, asking for specific help expresses need and vulnerability, which is a growth step. To make a request of the group is to bring something out from "behind the leaf." Give them some examples of how they might describe their fear and ask for help:

- "I am afraid of being judged. So when I share, I would like for someone to just tell me it's okay."

- "I am afraid of being judged. So when I share, I would like for you all just to be there and not give me feedback unless I ask for it. I just need to be accepted first."
- "I am afraid that no one will tell me the truth. So when I share, no matter how brutal or negative it is, I just want to know exactly what you think about it. Be honest with me."
- "Sometimes I need to know that God is with me, so when I share I might want someone to pray."

What *Being Known* Means

Give members some examples of what it means to *be known*, because they might wonder what parts of themselves they are to let others know. The ideal level of being known will vary. Even in the most surface-level groups, such as discussion groups, members are responsible at least to let others know their thoughts, reflections, or opinions on the topic or passage. In deeper groups they will share pain, feelings, fears, and struggles.

Your group and its purpose will dictate what is appropriate, but whatever that appropriateness is, members should know. Here are some things "beneath the leaf" that you might make them responsible to share:

Feelings	Desires	Needs
Attitudes	Loves	Wishes
Behaviors	Fears	Sexuality
Choices	Passions	Anger
Values	Losses	Hatred
Limits	Pains	Sin
Thoughts	Dreams	Failure
Tenderness	Confrontations	"Dark and ugly parts"
Giving	Hurts	Secrets
Sacrifice	Opinions	
Talents	Feedback for others	

Some of these are deeper and scarier than others, but all are part of being human. Whether an issue is okay to share will vary by group, but the general rule is, the more of oneself that is brought to relationship with others, the more knowing takes place. And the more knowing that occurs, the more change happens. When things are brought into the light, the Bible says, they become visible and Christ can shine on them (Ephesians 5:13–14).

To the extent that it is appropriate, model for your members how you want them to make themselves known. Some people have never seen anyone be real and open up to others. You can give them a snapshot of what it looks like through examples such as "I know what this is like. I feel very afraid sometimes in . . . situations" or "When I think of failure, it is not hard to come up with something. Just this morning, I. . . . Can anyone else relate to feeling that way?"

One time I (Henry) had an upsetting interchange right before I had to lead a group and did not have time to cool off. So I went into the group and asked, "What do you guys do when you feel like I do right now? I am so mad about something I just want to. . . ." They were a little shocked that their leader had such feelings, but I will never forget that group. For the next hour and a half people were more honest than I had ever experienced them, and it was because I as the leader had shown them what honesty and being known look like.

Taking Responsibility

Encourage each member to take responsibility for being known. Let the people know that there is a risk in group, as in life. Just as no one can live our lives for us, no one can be known for us. We have to do that ourselves. The extent to which members will grow is somewhat in their hands. It relates to how much they let the group "into their hearts" by "opening wide" (2 Corinthians 6:11–13).

Explain the payoff for taking responsibility to be known. Honesty and wellness are linked. To the extent that we are honest and known by others, not only do we have a better group experience, but we do better in life. The healthiest people are the most honest ones. "You are only as sick as your secrets" is an important truth. Letting people know this bib-lical value will help them move toward honesty.

Emphasize that good group experiences do not happen if members are not real. While you can do a lot to facilitate that, there is a limit to what you can do. *Let the members know their role.* Discuss how being known is their job and that you will try to help them to do that. But you can't do it for them, so they have to get to work and get real.

Chapter 38

Really Listen to Each Other

The important needs of knowing and being known are a big part of what it means to love and be loved. True connectedness and intimacy come as we know and love each other deeply. "Now that you have purified yourselves by obeying the truth so that you have sincere love for your brothers, love one another deeply, from the heart" (1 Peter 1:22).

For this to happen, we have to have a real understanding of each other as well as an experience of being understood. In other words, not only do we need to be known, but we need to know that we are known. That only comes from the art of listening to each other and knowing we have been heard. Simply said, it is the art of group members' empathy for each other. It is the task of really hearing each other and knowing this has happened. It is the art of "being with."

In many groups this does not happen. People do not listen to each other. Instead, they preach, teach, advise, pontificate, and immediately talk about themselves. All those things might have their place at some point, but usually they are way down the list of priorities, way behind the need to just listen.

As a group leader you can listen to people and express empathy to show that you really hear. (See chapter 26.) But it is also important that your group members listen to each other. Give it high ranking in the priorities of values for the group, and do what you can to facilitate its happening.

Orient Members to the Value of Listening

Model listening in verbal and nonverbal ways that validate and empathize. Point out these choices in the group orientation. Talk to the members about the value of listening to each other. Have members share their own difficulties in listening. Ask about their experiences in not being listened to. Do some education on barriers to listening and "listening felonies."

Give Feedback

Suggest giving feedback to each other if someone does not feel listened to. The person who doesn't feel listened to may let the hearer know what would have felt better. Find out if members want feedback from other members when they are not listening well. Make process statements about listening and check in with the group. "It seems that we are doing a lot of talking about experiences and giving opinions. How does everyone feel in terms of really being heard tonight?"

If your group has decided that it is okay, give the feedback yourself to the nonlistener. "Joe, I notice that when people start to talk about things that are difficult, you immediately give them advice. Have you noticed that? Why do you think you do that?" Again, these kinds of statements fall into the categories of what kind of group you've decided to have, but they can be huge in building intimacy and connectedness.

Intervene When Necessary

Take charge as a facilitator when someone is not listened to. You can interrupt in simple ways when someone is not listening. Simply say, "Wait, Joe. Let's make sure we let Susan finish."

You can also go further by saying, "I don't think we really finished with Sally." Then empathize, "Sally, it seems you were saying that you have felt really overwhelmed this week" or "I am not sure that was what she was saying, Tom. Sally, don't let us miss this. Tell us more."

The key is to reenter the experience where the person was before the failure in listening. By doing this you have corrected the nonlistener, saved the process, and also modeled to him and the group how to do better.

There are no real rules about all this, but there is a culture to a group, just as in any other relationship. The feeling of being listened to is one of the most important gifts we can give to each other. Do what you can to make sure that the group members understand this gift and try to grow in their ability to give it to each other as best they can.

Chapter 39

Give and Receive Feedback

I f you did a study on the value the Bible places on our being eyes and ears for each other, it would be an entire book in itself. As group members we need to receive feedback and know others' perceptions about us. Gaining correction and accurate self-perceptions is essential to growth and change. The Bible says we are responsible to give and receive feedback—both negative and positive. We cannot see ourselves accurately if we are not doing this for each other.

The Bible Values Feedback

One of the Bible's strongest messages is that we truly do need each other. Verse after verse explains that we need positive feedback, helpful correction and criticism, praise and affirmation, and more. This feedback helps us clarify how we understand our gifts, faults, and self-image. We must also give this benefit to others.

Here is a sample of what the Bible says about the value of giving each other feedback. Notice how it calls us to combine grace and truth in how we give and receive this important information.

Therefore each of you must put off falsehood and speak truthfully to his neighbor, for we are all members of one body (Ephesians 4:25).

Each one should use whatever gift he has received to serve others, faithfully administering God's grace in its various forms. If anyone speaks, he should do it as one speaking the very words of God (1 Peter 4:10–11).

We urge you, brothers, warn those who are idle, encourage the timid, help the weak, be patient with everyone (1 Thessalonians 5:14).

He who ignores discipline comes to poverty and shame, but whoever heeds correction is honored (Proverbs 13:18).

"Do not rebuke a mocker or he will hate you; rebuke a wise man and he will love you. Instruct a wise man and he will be wiser still; teach a righteous man and he will add to his learning" (Proverbs 9:8–9).

Brothers, if someone is caught in a sin, you who are spiritual should restore him gently (Galatians 6:1).

He who ignores discipline despises himself, but whoever heeds correction gains understanding (Proverbs 15.32).

"If your brother sins, rebuke him, and if he repents, forgive him" (Luke 17:3).

Therefore encourage one another and build each other up, just as in fact you are doing (1 Thessalonians 5:11).

As you can see, the Bible teaches that it is *our responsibility* to give and receive feedback. In fact, Leviticus 19:17 says that if you see something in someone yet fail to "rebuke your neighbor frankly," then you will "share in his guilt." Silence is not an option for a fully functioning

community, and therefore we see it as a real responsibility of a fully functioning group.

Benefits of Seeing Ourselves as Others Do

In the ideal group, members give and receive from each other. That
means an important task for you as a group member is to *know what
others know about you.* It is the task of hearing and receiving things from
others.

Groups observe so much. Other members' experience of us is valuable because they listen to us, see us, learn what it is like to be around
us, and observe us verbally and nonverbally. They evaluate our lives and
behavior. In a good group we lay ourselves open for observation, to varying degrees. Your group members should see it as their task to understand what the rest of the group sees about them regarding:

- Feelings, attitudes, values, and spirituality
- Behaviors, patterns, self-destructiveness, weaknesses, needs,
  and pain
- Limitations, pride, arrogance, and sinfulness
- Talents and abilities
- Communication and relational styles

Groups recognize our gifts. Many people grow up having significant relationships in which they're not evaluated accurately. They have
been called "bad" when they are not bad, or "selfish" when they are truly
giving, and so forth. A good group can give feedback that corrects those
distortions. Some people may even be unaware of gifts and abilities that
they possess and need others to tell them.

Groups help correct our faults. We can be out of touch with our
own sin, faults, and weaknesses. A person can easily be one who "flat-
ters himself too much to detect or hate his sin" (Psalm 36:2). The group
lets us know where we need to change when we do not see it.

Groups help match self-images to reality. The group can give us
feedback about life patterns we have never seen or been told of or even
have a clue about. Our self-image has much to do with how we fare in
life. Sometimes that view of ourselves is not the accurate picture the Bible

commands us to have (Romans 12:3). When the group gives us accurate feedback, we can get our picture of ourselves in touch with reality.

Balancing our self-image with reality comes from feedback in our relationships, and a good group is in a great position to give that kind of feedback. But it only can help if we have the wisdom to hear. So a member's task is to listen and take it to heart (Matthew 18:15; Proverbs 15:31). That is what a wise person does.

Deciding Whether to Be a Group That Gives Feedback

Granted, giving and receiving feedback affects a group's limitations, goals, and purposes. Feedback may not be appropriate to a particular group. It may even be counterproductive. But if you have decided to have the kind of group that gives feedback to each other, we think it is important for the members to understand their responsibility and do it well.

Why Some Groups Don't Allow Cross-Talk

The issue of giving feedback when a person shares something in the group is sometimes called *cross-talk*. Some who lead very successful groups allow no cross-talk. They think it takes away safety from the group and see most growth as coming from members being able to share without fearing what someone else might say.

These leaders believe their groups help people while avoiding the harm of feedback that is wrong, hurtful, inappropriate, or less than helpful. Advice giving, spiritualization, judgment, criticism, inappropriate agreement, and flattery can all make a group unsafe. Therefore some leaders believe that if you just stick to open sharing, good things will happen. And there is a lot of truth, experience, and track record to back that up. There is no doubt that this model is helpful, and we in no way are critical of it. It has been shown to bear much fruit, especially in recovery groups. For example, we work with a large church that uses our Foundations program with hundreds of people per week in small groups with no cross-talk. They are very effective in what they do with that model.

Some group members prefer a group like that because they want only support and feel too fragile to hear much input from others. Facilitators find that this takes off pressure for them to monitor feedback. Many people are afraid to be direct and honest, whether because of bad experiences or personal weakness. Those who can't see others clearly tend to give errant feedback, or they give it in a hurtful or non-useful way, often without grace or compassion. These potential problems make the no-feedback model particularly attractive in circles with minimally trained leaders, because it does not require as much work.

Accepting Feedback Responsibilities

However, we think that groups that limit feedback also limit our chances to experience—in community—receiving input, correction, confrontation, coaching, support, care, love, and empathy. Your members can experience the benefits of feedback if you prepare them to accept the value and receive it well.

Prepare your group. Affirm the value of feedback by giving its biblical context. Be strong on the values of kindness, compassion, humility, and gentleness. Remind members that feedback is not just for negative things they see, but also affirmation, encouragement, and prodding each other to grow. As Paul said, "For God did not give us a spirit of timidity, but a spirit of power, of love and of self-discipline" (2 Timothy 1:7). Encourage members to play their part in this helpful process.

Ask about their positive and negative experiences in "speaking the truth in love." Ask them to tell the group their fears, discomfort, and resistance to hearing from others. Learn whether members have difficulty either giving or receiving feedback. Talk about the importance of grace and truth going together.

See if they would like to adopt receiving feedback as a group value. Talk about how each wants it done so that members know how to do it for each other. Have them share the areas in which they feel they need the most feedback. What helps them experience grace when they are being given feedback? Ask if they would like to set any ground rules.

Receive feedback responsibly. Help them to see feedback as a gift from the group, a chance to build wisdom, a key to success in every area of life. When members experience difficulty in giving or receiving honest feedback within the group, tie that to the same difficulties they have in the outside world. Ask them if they have ever known anyone who could not receive feedback. What was it like to be with that person? Show them that the group can be a place to learn and practice a new skill of being more direct and honest with others.

Model how to receive feedback. Don't get defensive, justify yourself, or devalue the feedback. Just receive it as a gift. Develop an attitude of desiring truth, even if it is uncomfortable. Ask for feedback in relation to what you are doing.

Combining grace and truth also means that you or they may be evaluative of the feedback received. What one receives is not necessarily true, so you or they should evaluate it from an open stance. All should be nonreactive to other members when it is given. No one should be punished for saying something that is tough to hear. The goal is to stay connected and in the moment, not moving away from the relationship when the confrontation comes.

As facilitator, when you see someone observing another, invite the observer to share what she is seeing. "Susie, tell us what you are thinking about what Sally has shared. Do you have any observations for her?" Invite the group to do the same thing. "Does anyone have any feedback for Tom?" This growth step helps members enhance their skills. "What was that like for you, Tom, to say that to Susan?" Allow the members to process giving feedback and then to use the group to give them feedback on their giving feedback. "What did the group think about how Tom did that?"

Obviously, not all groups go as deep as some of these suggestions imply. But the most life-changing groups do go this deep. So, if this is the kind of group you are developing, your group members' role includes taking ownership of their stance toward feedback so that things work well. You cannot receive feedback for them, but you can try to facilitate their "catching the bug." God has given us each other to help us see life, him, and ourselves more accurately. That can only happen if everyone does his job. Help your members do theirs!

Chapter 40

Learn to Love

I f you as a small group leader had the opportunity to ask Jesus face to face what should be your group's most important focus, what do you think he would say? It is not a stretch to say that actually happened one day.

Hearing that Jesus had silenced the Sadducees, the Pharisees got together. One of them, an expert in the law, tested him with this question: "Teacher, which is the greatest commandment in the Law?"

Jesus replied: "'Love the Lord your God with all your heart and with all your soul and with all your mind.' This is the first and greatest commandment. And the second is like it: 'Love your neighbor as yourself.' All the Law and the Prophets hang on these two commandments" (Matthew 22:34–40).

If all of life rests on the two commandments of loving God and loving others, it seems that doing both in a small group would be a good idea. In fact, we see three very important reasons for trying to make this happen in small groups. First, it is the best experience that people can get to help them for the things they came to the group seeking help for. No matter what ails us, the love of God and the love of others can help cure us. Second, if members are "doing" these things as well as receiving them, then the group has become a healing agent. Third, if they are learning how to love God and others in your group, the members will take it to the outside world and pass it on. Thus, their marriages, parenting, dating, work life, and everything else will improve. So the question becomes, how do you get the group involved in the Great Commandment?

Loving God

Have your members see in how many ways they can fulfill their responsibility to show their love for God.

- Relate to him directly in the group through worship and prayer.
- Lift him up as the Source of life and answers.
- Learn his ways and design for life.
- Work on obeying his commandments and spur one another on to do that.
- Love one another and thus obey his Great Commandment.
- Bring into the group experience all of the different aspects of life, thus giving him reign of heart, mind, soul, and strength.
- Develop the image of God in the group members, growing in all aspects of being a person.
- Take risks in putting one's talents to use and thus bearing fruit for him.
- Make the group a place of light where people can bring everything into the Light of God.
- Make the group a place of confession and repentance.
- Serve one another.
- Do group service together.

- Find ways to bring whatever you are doing under his lordship and have it seen as celebrating the spiritual life.

Loving Each Other

You can help your group become equally creative in fulfilling their responsibilities to love each other.

- Give empathy.
- Offer encouragement.
- Tell each other the truth.
- Affirm each other.
- Support one another.
- Validate each other's strengths and talents.
- Spur one another on toward growth and risk taking.
- Accept the different parts of each other as they are expressed and thus help each other become more whole.
- Love and accept the unlovable parts of each other.
- Accept each other's failures.
- Confess to each other.
- Offer and receive forgiveness.
- Give to one another things that one's family did not provide.
- Pray for one another.
- Confront one another.
- Model and teach one another.
- Discipline one another.
- Weep with each other and help grief and loss.
- Touch each other's wounded parts and pain.
- Contain each other's sin.
- Hold each other accountable.
- Disciple one another.
- Develop unity of spirit and oneness with one another.
- Bind your hearts together with love through vulnerability.
- Serve one another.

- Show patience with one another.
- Bear each other's burdens.

Moving from Lists to Actions

All these items come directly from the New Testament. As a facilitator you might want to construct experiences that can make these things happen or find materials that do. You can also bring up these items with the group, asking, "How well do you think we as a group are showing love in these ways?"

Next, you want to get the group members to be both on the giving and receiving end of loving one another. It's powerful when a group leader notices that a member is giving, for example, and not receiving very much. Think of what would happen if you made a process statement like, "Sally, I have noticed something. You are so empathic to others' struggles in the group. But when people offer help to you, you quickly turn it around to helping them again. Maybe it is time for the group to give to you tonight. What can we help you with?"

Remember, a facilitator monitors the process to see what is happening in the group. Is there someone who is giving the love of God but not experiencing it? It is your job to keep the group balanced.

So—and this is key—for all the members to both give and receive, they must be vulnerable. They have to come out of hiding. How can they experience encouragement if they never share anything that requires courage? How can they experience anyone weeping with them (Romans 12:15) if they never experience sadness in the group? Granted, not all groups go to all these places, but remember this about the body's work: for members to do what the Bible says for one another, there has to be "another." This means that whenever someone is giving, someone is vulnerably receiving. It is your job to make sure that humility, vulnerability, and brokenness are expressed and experienced, or none of this will go below the surface.

Leaders can also cast a vision for these things in the group culture. You might begin with sharing what you want to happen over the course of the group. Let them know that you desire a group where they can experience God's love and give and receive love with one another in its various forms. Then you can use the above lists to orient them to what love looks like.

Also, you are a powerful model for what you want the group to understand. As they see you living out these things in your interventions with the group, they will get it. When you extend empathy, for example, they will see what it looks like and that it is appropriate for the group. Then they will most likely begin to do it. If they don't, since you have shown them, you will be on more solid ground to get a good response when you say, "Does anyone have a response to what Tom just shared?" If you have shown honest feedback, confrontation, or support, they will have somewhere to go.

Remember that showing love is each member's responsibility. You are not the source of all of these things for all of them. You are the facilitator to help them fulfill their role as the body who does all of these things for each other (Ephesians 4:16). So don't get caught up in the role of the provider. Make sure you are facilitating their experience of these commandments in the ways we listed. Teach, encourage, model, facilitate, orient, present, observe, and comment—but, ultimately, remember that it is their group and their job!

Chapter 41

Practice Obedience

A valuable role that members in good groups learn to take on is the good old-fashioned concept of *obedience*. Biblically defined as *yielding*, obedience means that we submit and adapt to God's truths, from whatever source he presents. His Word, his Spirit, and his people are the main sources. Though it requires humility and giving up self-will, God designed obedience for our own good and blessing: "The LORD commanded us to obey all these decrees and to fear the LORD our God, so that we might always prosper and be kept alive, as is the case today" (Deuteronomy 6:24). Rather than seeing obedience as deprivation, control, or punishment, God means it as the path to his Promised Land of love, freedom, and life.

Obedience Is for Our Good

The benefits of obedience are best learned through suffering, which was the way of Jesus: "Although he was a son, he learned obedience from what he suffered" (Hebrews 5:8). In the same manner, group members learn that taking risks, opening up their hearts to each other, and giving and receiving feedback, though often uncomfortable and scary, bring forth good fruit in their lives and relationships.

Obedience also helps members integrate themselves with the rest of the group. A commitment to follow God and his ways of growth builds a sense of alliance. It also creates safety as members share a common allegiance to biblical principles that develop growth and health. And obedience helps members see the value of humility and submission; we were not designed to be God, answering only to ourselves. We were made to follow him, and our lives work better when we take on that role.

Obedience Involves the Whole Person

In good groups, members learn to experience the reality that *obedience is both internal and external; it involves the whole person.* In other words, there are realities, statutes, and principles that we are to yield to, in both our behavior and the deepest recesses of our hearts. When Jesus confronted the leaders, he included both as areas to be obeyed, though he also taught that one was more important than the other:

> "Woe to you, teachers of the law and Pharisees, you hypocrites! You give a tenth of your spices—mint, dill and cummin. But you have neglected the more important matters of the law—justice, mercy and faithfulness. You should have practiced the latter, without neglecting the former" (Matthew 23:23).

> Then the Lord said to them, "Now then, you Pharisees clean the outside of the cup and dish, but inside you are full of greed and wickedness. You foolish people! Did not the one who made the outside make the inside also?" (Luke 11:39–40).

Often you will see one aspect of obedience neglected in a group setting. One group type will concentrate solely on members' acting out and objective behaviors. The other will be concerned only with its members' relationships, emotional honesty, and presence. Both aspects, however, are necessary, because they perform different roles for the group members. The rules concerning external obedience function as a protective structure. They give a guide and framework to the group, so that people's hearts and feelings are not in jeopardy or disrupted. For example, dishonoring the commitment to attend, be on time, and follow group rules would create chaos and impede the process. The rules concerning matters of the heart keep members' souls attuned to staying in the process. Being just, merciful, and faithful creates love, trust, and growth in the members.

Helping Members Practice Obedience

There are several ways you can help members assume their roles as obedient servants of Christ.

Teach them that obedience is for their good. Many people come to a group believing that obedience is something God requires for his benefit, not theirs. Help members see that obedience brings blessings to us. You might say, "I think that our meeting here is one of the ways we obey God, and that there is a reason that this is good for us. What sorts of goals and expectations do you have about embarking on this obedience?"

Help them see that obedience involves the inside. Obedience involves both behaviors and heart. Your members can really help each other with both sides of the equation. One person may say, "Randy, when you brought up your drinking problem, you were really concerned that it is wrong and a sin. However, you never mentioned how you feel about it, what you think might be causing it, or why you haven't brought it up to us until now. I think we want to know that part of you as well."

Help them see that obedience involves the external as well. By contrast, you might say in another situation, "Sandra has brought up that she is in an emotional affair, but since it's not physical, she thinks it's okay. I don't agree with that opinion, and I would like other members' feedback here."

Fall Back on Grace

Finally, group members learn a wonderful lesson as they commit to obeying God. They see we all need grace, forgiveness, and restoration. Show them how to depend on grace: "Ross, I can tell you feel pretty bad about getting too angry with your son. Why don't you ask the group how they feel about you right now, and see if there is condemnation or grace for you?"

Chapter 42

Make Positive Changes

I (John) was involved in many groups for my training as a psychologist in contrast with groups for my personal growth. In one training group, the leader believed that insight was the only curing element that really mattered. He thought that if people truly understood why they did what they did, they would change and heal, and the issues would be resolved. So we psychologists in training were to provide perception and feedback but not tell people what we thought they should do. An experience in the group taught me that this was not the best way to achieve our goals.

Insight Is Not Enough to Produce Change

I remember when Laurie brought up her intentions to have an affair. She was conflicted about it but thought it was the best thing to do. It was obviously a grave issue for Laurie and the group. There was a lot of emotion and empathy for her situation. People also spent time trying to help her understand her own issues, motives, and influences regarding this very destructive decision.

Finally one man said, "Laurie, I really care about you a lot, but I want to be clear with you that I don't think you should do this. It's wrong, and it will hurt a lot of people." It sort of shocked her, and she felt somewhat offended, as if he had no right to say this. Weeks later, however, Laurie told him, "I have been thinking about this whole thing, and I want to thank you for what you said. It's helped clear my mind, and I'm going a different direction now."

I remember learning from that group experience that insight and truth are very, very valuable. I also remember learning that *insight alone is not enough;* the result is paralysis of analysis, where change doesn't happen. Rather, the truth we learn and receive in relationships is designed to be used, applied, and lived out so that we may be transformed. This principle is stated no better than in James's words:

> Do not merely listen to the word, and so deceive yourselves. Do what it says. Anyone who listens to the word but does not do what it says is like a man who looks at his face in a mirror and, after looking at himself, goes away and immediately forgets what he looks like. But the man who looks intently into the perfect law that gives freedom, and continues to do this, not forgetting what he has heard, but doing it— he will be blessed in what he does (James 1:22–25).

All group members are responsible to take the stance that *the truth is to be both learned and used,* thereby moving down that famous eighteen inches between head and heart.

Sources of Truth

We do not possess all the truth we need. God provides it from sources that he provides in several areas. Here are some of the ways to find valuable realities that can help our lives.

When others have experienced a member's actions, speech, and attitudes, they give **feedback** that is a valuable source of information for each other. When a member becomes aware of an emotion, reaction, or pattern in his **own experience,** he often has an "aha" moment;

this indicates he is observing himself within the group. Also, members often learn much about themselves by **observing others** to see how they interact with group members.

Principles, such as propositional truths, concepts, and biblical realities, help people see how truth affects their lives and relationships. In some cases a person may only be able to receive truth about himself by experiencing the **consequences** of pain or loss through the discipline process.

Apply the Truth

Once members are engaged in the search for truth about themselves, they also need to know how to use and apply it in ways that heal, restore, and mature them. Here are some ways to make truth useful and usable.

Help members verbalize issues. Members are truly helped when they can articulate what they are learning about themselves. An experience can be powerful and healing, but an experience that can be translated into a concept about one's issues is even better. The person can then take that experience, generalize it, observe it in her daily life, and take responsibility for it.

For example, while leading a group I said, "Glenn, almost every time someone gives you feedback, you seem to regard it as an attack, and you miss people's caring underneath it." He came back week after week with reports on how often he did that in his marriage, his parenting, and his job. That observation was a tool he used to understand himself better and change.

Show them how to notice patterns. When the group helps identify patterns and realities in a person, they function as a safe laboratory for the person to see these patterns in operation. As we said, just because someone has the insight doesn't mean he will change immediately. But when everyone is in on the issue, they can point out instances. The members and the person talk about their responses when they see the pattern played out in the group. In the example above, a group member might tell Glenn, "I think it's happening again. I am trying to say something, and I feel shut out from you. What's going on?"

Assign tasks for growth. Group members are responsible to use the truth to make necessary adjustments that result in life change. They learn their issues and specific, individual tasks to resolve them. The isolated person may have the task of talking from the heart and letting people in. The rescuer might have the job of allowing someone to feel discomfort and to be present with him without attempting to fix him. The impulsive person may work on putting actions into symbols and words. For example, a group member or facilitator might ask, "Now that Fran is aware of how she tends to eat or spend money when she is sad, what are some things she can do when she feels the tension?" (Good sources for identifying and working on these tasks are our books *Changes That Heal* and *Hiding from Love*.)

Evaluate whether truth is working. The group members help each other see whether they're progressing in the areas of concern. The right conditions for progress include a heart to grow, on-target understanding, and necessary resources. If these elements are present, change should occur over time. Members help monitor in a noncritical and humble way whether people seem to produce good fruit or furrow the same ground again without result. When growth is slow, someone might comment, "Robin, it seems that no matter what feedback the group gives you, your struggles with your daughter don't change. Can anyone give Robin some feedback on what they think might be going on?"

Make truth a friend of the group, and see it change lives and experiences.

Chapter 43

Learn New Skills

Groups are about growth. By definition, members in an effective group will become "more" of something. Hopefully, they will become more loving, honest, effective in living life, knowledgeable of God, and intimate with him and others. In the book *Safe People* we said that a "safe person" is a person who helps us do three things:

- Get closer to God
- Get closer to others
- Get closer to becoming the person God created us to be

In other words, as a result of being with good people, we should be growing into a deeper and more meaningful relationship with God, deeper and more meaningful relationships with other people, and a greater fulfilling of our own created identity. Growth is about all of life.

Right Mind-set Leads to Action

We think that the same three growth directions happen in a good group. Becoming "more" of the persons who are closer to God, others, and their created identities means that members have to do new things, have new experiences, and learn new skills.

Time to Try New Things

Therefore members must accept a role and responsibility to try new things in the group. As these new experiences, skills, and learning become part of who they are, members take new things to the outside world. In chapter 36, "Expect the Unexpected," we talked about a mind-set. Now we are talking about actually "getting out of the boat." It is the fruit of the earlier mind-set. It is the "works that prove one's faith" part of the group experience. Consider the words of James:

> You foolish man, do you want evidence that faith without deeds is useless? Was not our ancestor Abraham considered righteous for what he did when he offered his son Isaac on the altar? You see that his faith and his actions were working together, and his faith was made complete by what he did. And the scripture was fulfilled that says, "Abraham believed God, and it was credited to him as righteousness," and he was called God's friend. You see that a person is justified by what he does and not by faith alone (James 2:20–24).

In other words, it's good to have faith that God will grow me in a group. But to actually "work" or have "actions" in that group is another thing. Members who take risks in the group and do new things there will grow the most. Being active in the growth process is each member's role and responsibility.

Group can be a very powerful laboratory in which people get their first opportunity to learn certain life skills. If used correctly, group can be, for example, the family environment where members learn to relate in ways that their original families never taught them. Old patterns can be changed as people learn new ways of being in this new family of God. But that requires that they actually do new things.

Each Member Is Responsible to Grow

You cannot do these things for the members any more than a parent can walk for a child. Neither can the other group members. And neither will God. Each member is responsible to take active steps for his or her own growth. As Paul says, "Work out your salvation with fear and trembling, for it is God who works in you to will and to act according to his good purpose" (Philippians 2:12–13). God and others can help, but each one must also carry his own load of growth and compare his growth work only with himself (Galatians 6:4–5).

Create an Environment for Growth

Although you cannot do the stretching and growing for your members, as facilitator you create an environment for growth. To develop and facilitate each member's growth, you will want to cast a vision, help members commit to developing specific skills, and nurture an atmosphere of safety and grace.

Cast a Vision

Cast a vision for "active growth" in the group. You might do this in orientation, as part of each meeting's preparation time, and as an ongoing process. Share with them that you want the group to be a place where they get to try new things and grow in new skills with each other.

Work on developing a culture within the group wherein staying the same, or not trying new things, is against the norm. Remember, a group enforces its own norms. If it is a high value of the culture to try new things and stretch oneself, then when someone is not doing that, the group will let her know.

Cast the vision of the group being God's family, and thus a new family where he grows us up and we learn all the things we did not learn the first time around (Ephesians 4:15–16).

Commit to Developing Specific Skills

Ask the group to share with the group the new skills they would learn and try. In what things do they need practice or stretching? Offer some examples of areas where they can be stretched to maturity or completeness (Hebrews 6:1). Here are some examples of new skills and experiences that people can use in group to learn and grow:

- Share feelings openly
- Share struggles
- Confess weakness, failure, or sin
- Share pain and grief
- Receive love and comfort
- Express fear
- Confront others
- Be honest about what they think
- Deal with anger
- Be assertive
- Express wishes, needs, and desires
- Experience intimacy
- Pray and share their spiritual sides
- Be held accountable
- Express kindness and tenderness or affection
- Discover, try, or display talents
- Openly dream about what could be
- Resolve conflict with others
- Express and receive forgiveness
- Be nurtured
- Nurture others
- Listen
- Depend on others
- Depend on God
- Give up control
- Take control
- Make goals and expectations and be held to them
- Receive correction and feedback without defensiveness
- Submit
- Give up duplicity and be authentic
- Be present and congruent with who they truly are

Get the members to share with the others what new skills they would like to be held accountable for within the group. Ask how they want that accountability to be structured.

Emphasize Safety and Grace

Develop your group as a safe atmosphere that offers grace during failure and learning. Talk about the value of taking baby steps. Emphasize the need to accept each other even when you don't get it right.

Give the members permission to ask each other for help they need in taking the next step. Encourage them to push each other toward taking those steps (Hebrews 10:24). Make process statements about how they are doing in this regard. You might say:

- "I notice that opening up in that way is something new for you. That was great! What was it like for you?"
- "What were some of the group's responses to his taking that step?"
- "I notice that you are not doing with us what you said you want to learn how to do. What is going on?"
- "This seems like a good opportunity to do what you said you wanted to learn how to do. Why don't you tell the group how you are feeling with what is happening at work?"

There is no right or wrong process statement. It just has to fit what is going on and facilitate a next step.

Remember, growth is the members' job. Facilitating that growth is yours. Cast the vision, and try to make the culture one where next steps take place. Then watch what God does!

Chapter 44

Discover and Develop Gifts

I (John) was leading a growth group in which Chip became embroiled in angry confrontation with several members. Chip had been very direct—actually harsh—with Nancy, and the others were mad at him for hurting her feelings. He thought he had been appropriate and felt they were ganging up on him and overprotecting Nancy.

I didn't intervene at this point because the group had been meeting for some time and were maturing together. I wanted to see how the "family" handled this dispute on its own, without "Dad" coming in as judge and jury.

At first it wasn't working well. People were entrenched in their positions and opinions. The confronting members were frustrated with Chip's recalcitrance. His anger escalated. However, during a few seconds' pause, while everyone was trying to figure out what to do next, Donna, who had not been involved, looked at Chip and said quietly, "This has got to be so hard for you right now."

Almost instantly, tears welled in Chip's eyes and he softened. Things calmed down in the room. Chip started talking about how, when he was a kid and disagreed with his parents, the whole family always came down on him, no matter who was right or wrong. He carried the feeling that if he expressed his own opinion, everyone would gang up on him. Soon the group got more connected to Chip, and we could safely look at his earlier interaction with Nancy without further reactions.

Donna manifested her gift of insight by reaching out to Chip. She had the ability to look beneath the obvious and understand that, though she didn't know Chip's story, he was hurt and alienated underneath the anger. Donna's talent served the members many times throughout the group's life.

Giving Is Part of Growing

When members take responsibility to discover, develop, and use their gifts and talents to help others, they experience healing. It sounds ironic that helping others helps us, and it is true that those with rescuing and enabling tendencies must become aware of when their giving to others works against their need to receive. But ultimately, the group operates as a microcosm of the body of Christ. Everyone receives, everyone gives, and hopefully everyone grows and benefits: "From him the whole body, joined and held together by every supporting ligament, grows and builds itself up in love, as each part does its work" (Ephesians 4:16).

The Purpose of Gifts

God designed us with unique abilities, talents, and gifts, all meant to help others.

Now to each one the manifestation of the Spirit is given for the common good (1 Corinthians 12:7).

Since you are eager to have spiritual gifts, try to excel in gifts that build up the church (1 Corinthians 14:12).

Each one should use whatever gift he has received to serve others, faithfully administering God's grace in its various forms (1 Peter 4:10).

This last reference teaches that when group members apply their gifts to each other, they are actually delivering God's grace to others' hearts and lives, which transforms and changes people from the inside out. As we said in chapter 1, this is truly Plan A for growth, not Plan B.

Growth and Gifts

The saying goes, "Character is more important than giftedness." That is certainly true. A mature and less talented person is better off to himself and others than a highly gifted and characterless individual. At the same time, discovering and using abilities in the group affects the growth process itself in very significant ways. For example, part of emotional maturity is *discovering that you matter, can contribute, and are useful and valuable to others.* When people don't feel they have anything to offer, they often think of themselves as dead wood, cut off from humanity. Many people in groups find new life, as Donna did, when they realize they have a special ability that assists others.

As people mature and heal in their groups, they tend to become more aware of talents and abilities. They are safer, freer to take risks, and better able to look inside themselves and to hear the perceptions of others. Growth and gifts go hand in hand.

Being Aware

Some groups engage in a formal process to learn what their members' gifts are, and that is valuable. Yet a general growth group can simply use the meeting process to begin noticing special abilities. This tends to occur pretty much in the present. Group members have a dual role in being aware of their own emerging gifts and noticing others' gifts. As people become involved and connected, their talents begin to operate. Members need to make sure they bring up when they notice these gifts, so the gifted person becomes aware.

Here are a few gifts and abilities that may emerge as groups operate in love and truth:

- *Emotional presence:* being able to "be there" with someone who is in distress or pain

- *Compassion and empathy:* being able to experience someone's emotional state
- *Knowledge:* having specific information about a subject, as with someone who understands addictions or family issues
- *Wisdom and insight:* having the ability to see patterns underneath the surface and provide helpful truth
- *Discernment:* having the ability to sense when someone is being evasive or dishonest and helping him correct

Tips on Helping Members with Gifts

So far in this book we have talked a lot about growth as revealing wounded parts so we can regain the wholeness God intends for us. Members may feel encouraged to focus also on the positive results of recognizing hidden talents.

Open them up to gifts as part of group growth. Help them see that group is not only about learning, struggle, and process, but also about discovering and developing gifts. Say something like, "As we get to know each other, we will notice not only one another's struggles, but also each other's talents. When you see one, mention it to the group, as someone may not even be aware she has that strength."

Offer examples. Using the list above, identify some of the strengths people will manifest in group, so they can have a framework for noting gifts in themselves and other members.

Model awareness of gifts. Let members learn how to do this as they observe you. You might say, "Cheryl, you showed a lot of empathy for Jason when he talked about his parents' divorce. That gift is a good thing, and I am glad you are bringing this part of yourself to the group."

Help them encourage one another. Make it a norm that members show each other how they are helped by their gifts. For example, "Margaret, when you noticed that Lynn gets anxious when we talk about conflict, that was really helpful to her and the group. How has anyone else benefited from Margaret's gift of insight?"

Make sure all members seek to know their own and other's special contributions as they grow together.

Chapter 45

Discern Harmful Patterns

One of the things driving many people to group involvement is that they often have ineffective patterns of living and coping. These patterns don't come out of nowhere. More likely, they have come from experiences and struggles over a long period of time in their lives. Groups have an important task in helping their members give up the old and grow into the new.

Groups have to do with learning and experiencing a new way of life, which is in great contrast to what the Bible calls a *former way:*

> You were taught, with regard to your former way of life, to put off your old self, which is being corrupted by its deceitful desires; to be made new in the attitude of your minds; and to put on the new self, created to be like God in true righteousness and holiness (Ephesians 4:22–24).

That is, the old patterns of life did not work; life broke down in some areas—as it should—when we are out of control, away from God's paths, or alienated. The corrupt old ways, which we were never designed to live, are to be put away so that we can put on the new self, the one that is created by God and is like him.

Dig into Old Ways

That is why digging into old ways and patterns is helpful for people in the group. They need to identify, repent of, work through, and put aside the old way. If they let go of nothing, they will experience no change, ownership, or growth. The new way cannot be entered.

Some people get concerned that understanding the past leads a person only to lay blame and externalize responsibility. These concerned people want to "start afresh today." It's true that group members must be aware of tendencies to live in the past and avoid present ownership and choices. To do so would be to avoid repentance. In fact, looking at the past and turning from it is the essence of repentance itself. But if we ignore past patterns, we lose much-needed information that God makes available to us. The New Testament teaches regarding the lessons of Israel's past: "These things happened to them as examples and were written down as warnings for us, on whom the fulfillment of the ages has come" (1 Corinthians 10:11).

These are some of the former ways members might have handled their lives:

- *Self-sufficiency:* attempting to be strong and meet my needs by myself
- *Emotional deadness:* ignoring my pain until it cannot be accessed
- *Self-judgment:* harsh messages to myself about failure, to keep me from reaching out to relationship
- *Rescue:* projecting into others what I need and giving it to them instead of receiving it for myself
- *Wrong people:* investing in people whose character offers little good to my growth and well-being
- *Isolation:* avoiding relating to people at deeper levels

- *Substances and harmful activities:* substituting harmful behaviors for the comfort, freedom, or power I should derive from relationship
- *Self-effort:* working and performing harder when I fail, rather than going to grace, help, and forgiveness

When group members recognize these aspects of how they tried to survive, they can then support each other in giving grace for failures. One might say to another, "I see why you stayed isolated all your life; you were afraid of being hurt" or "Your addiction seems to be the only way you used to think you had any choices."

Discover Ways to Gain New Life

Many group members do not enter the process with a clear-cut map of how they handled their needs or conflicts. They have not had opportunity, motivation, or safety to do so. Additionally, for many the former ways are also the present ways. They are still discovering how they stay away from authentic connection and vulnerability. Here are some tips to help group members unearth those hurtful patterns, in order to gain the new life.

Help them see their own past patterns. Encourage members to tie their past with their present so that they can see the relationship. For example, you might say, "Cindy, you have told us how hard it is to let people down or disappoint them. Were there any past relationships in which you think that problem might have started?"

Help them help each other. When people begin to open up about their past, other members are able to note events and patterns the individual may not have been aware of. Often people will review their childhood, relationships with their parents and significant people, personal losses or traumatic events, and the like. Sharing adult history—such as marriage and parenting issues, friendships, habits, and work matters— can be helpful as well. This might help a member observe, "When you describe how emotionally unavailable your mom was, it helps me understand how withdrawn you are."

See the past in the present. It is valuable when group members observe and comment on patterns within the group itself and find themes that run from now to then. For example, one person may say, "Sometimes you seem to try to keep everybody happy when it's obvious that you yourself aren't doing well. It helps make sense to me how you talked about having an alcoholic depressed dad that you had to cheer up as a kid." Having made that connection to the old ways, the member might now bring things back to a suggested new way for the present: "But as for me, I would feel much closer to you if you let me in on how badly you feel now, instead of worrying about taking care of me. What's going on?"

Learn from others. Members can derive a great deal of wisdom and insight as they listen to and identify with each other's stories of unhealthy relationship patterns. This is a benefit that only group can provide—the multiplicity of lives and themes, shared to help one another.

Discuss results of old ways. When members talk about how their old patterns affected their lives, it helps everyone to be aware of the emptiness or destructiveness of those ways. Understanding that these ways are not effective for meeting needs or solving problems helps people move away from them and seek out righteous, healthy ways. For example, a member might say, "The more I tried to be perfect and keep things together, the more I messed up my good relationships and the more I attracted people who needed me to be ideal for them. I ended up lonelier than ever."

Encourage members not to fear the old patterns, but bring them into relationship, face them, understand why they existed, and find new ways that bring good fruit into their lives. In this practice, God makes room for what he has for the members: "See, I am doing a new thing! Now it springs up; do you not perceive it? I am making a way in the desert and streams in the wasteland" (Isaiah 43:19).

Chapter 46

Confess and Repent

When we began the book, we talked about needing "anchors" to keep yourself from drifting while leading a small group. That way you know that no matter what is going on, you are not getting swept out to sea. No matter what kind of group you are leading, if certain things are happening, you know you are doing well. These anchors include helping people to see and experience:

- God as their source
- Relationship as their primary need in life
- Grace and forgiveness
- God as the boss
- His ways to live
- God in control of the world, themselves in control of themselves

These experiences form the foundation of the ministry of reconciliation in real life. They help members grow.

Having said that, we want to offer two "sub-anchors" or anchoring tasks for the wonderful world of small group leadership. If your group members are doing these two tasks—confession and repentance—then you are doing something very well as a small group leader. And your group is also more likely to be experiencing the anchors listed above.

Confession Produces Powerful Growth

Confessing where we miss the mark is one of the most powerful growth exercises available to humans. The sad thing is that most people think only of confessing their sins to God. They read 1 John 1:9, confess their sin to God, claim forgiveness from him, and move on. And that is very important. But it is not the whole picture of what the Bible prescribes.

The Bible also tells us of the tradition, the power, and the imperative to confess with and to each other. In the Old Testament, the Israelites came together to confess their sins and the sins of their fathers. They confessed the generational patterns before them and the ways that they were falling short themselves.

The New Testament says confess to each other and pray for one another for healing to occur. "Therefore confess your sins to each other and pray for each other so that you may be healed. The prayer of a righteous man is powerful and effective" (James 5:16).

When we do this in a group, powerful things happen:

- We see God as the source of forgiveness.
- We see God as the boss.
- We get much more deeply connected to each other as the fig leaf is removed.
- We experience and internalize the grace and acceptance of the group.
- We feel more of God's grace and love as a result of the group's grace.
- We are less alienated and more trusting.
- We are less ashamed and feel more like everyone else.

- We take responsibility for our actions and take a step toward self-control.
- We are humbled in a good way.

Repentance Takes Growth to the Next Level

It is incredible what this one act, confession, does for us. When we add repentance, then the process of growth within groups gets even more powerful.

- We get a change of mind about the seriousness of our sin.
- We submit at a deeper level to the "bosshood" of God and his lordship.
- We get a new direction that is less self-destructive.
- We are held accountable before the group.
- We gain a new understanding of God's ways.
- The destruction stops.
- We develop self-control and impulse control.
- We go down a path of living out his commandments and thus realize the truth that sets us free.
- We get more connected to each other in a supportive role to maintain our repentance and lean on each other.

In other words, these two simple disciplines powerfully move us toward reconciliation of the creation.

Putting Confession and Repentance in Your Process

Your members do well to know that confession and repentance can cause great gains in their group process. Here are eight tips to help them along that path:

1. Talk in the orientation, if appropriate for your group, about the value of confession and repentance. Basically you ask them to agree with the truth (confession) about ourselves and to have a change of mind and direction about something (repentance.) Talks about confession and repentance are almost synonyms for

a good group. In other words, we will come together, take a look at ourselves, see where we are missing the mark, and make some changes.

2. Take the concepts out of religious language and make them friendly. "Let's talk about where we are *missing the mark*, which is what *sin* really means, and want to do better. What have you seen that you want to talk about and change?"

3. Talk about the kinds of safety and grace necessary for a group that includes confession and repentance in its growth process.

4. Ask them to share their fears and resistances to confessing and repenting before a group. What has been their experience?

5. Ask them to talk about what they need from the present group to feel comfortable confessing and repenting.

6. Talk about a structure to confess and repent. Will it be a part of the ongoing nature of the discussions? In other words, as you study content, will you just say as you want to, "I can see where I fall short here"? Or will it be more structured, such as planning a time in the group for confession and repentance?

7. What about forgiveness? How does the group want to convey God's forgiveness to each other? How will they represent his priesthood? (1 Peter 2:9).

8. In their repentance, how would they like to be helped? How would they like to be held accountable? How would they like to be supported in their changes?

These are simple concepts. But they are powerful. Encourage your group members to see themselves as confessors and repenters and also as expressions of God's grace to each other. If that happens, all of you will find two good tasks that connect you to the anchors of reconciliation.

Chapter 47

Take Risks

Members of good groups adopt the stance that *risks are normal and expected*. Risk is an essential part of group and produces great effects in people. I (John) have seen people with smaller problems who took little risks and received little benefit. And I have seen people with huge problems who took great risks, and they ended up much better off than those in the first group.

I remember conducting a group that included a mature, professional person, much respected by the other members. Yet he was so intent on getting his spiritual and emotional work done that he would sometimes collapse into heaving, wracking, almost uncontrollable sobs as he dealt with his past. Like a little baby, he stained his shirt with tears. His face flushed. His nose ran. A couple of group members were discomfited by this and didn't know what to do. He was just too emotional for them. The rest of the group had deep compassion for him and respected him all the more for what he was doing. As for the man himself, he received great fruits for his risks. He was able to resolve many issues and today is living a meaningful life as a husband, father, successful businessman, and active church member.

When group members take risks, they expose themselves to the possibility of being hurt or embarrassed for the sake of taking a growth step. Like the professional man, they go through discomfort to gain a higher good. They step out of their comfort zone and try something they are afraid to do or experience. Like a person in physical therapy with a stiff and injured limb, they begin to take action to promote healing.

The result can be amazing. People begin to open up, become emotionally available and present, love truth instead of avoiding it, and become freer. These results also translate into many life changes in external circumstances, such as marriage, dating, friendships, parenting, and careers.

Provide Appropriate Safety for Appropriate Risk

The group's job is to provide an environment that is safe enough for a person to take risks that may be uncomfortable but not harmful or dangerous. If something is easy for a member, there is little risk and little growth. For example, the codependent man who reaches out in compassion to someone is doing a good—but for him probably not risky— thing. His risk might be to give someone some truthful feedback instead.

There is also such a thing as too much risk. For example, a woman who becomes so anxious that she can't think straight when she enters intense conflict with others may need to take very gradual small steps. She may first need to learn to feel safe in the presence of people who are having conflict, without engaging in it herself. That in itself may be a major growth step for her.

However—and this is important—*safety does not exist for its own sake in the group. It exists to promote growth and risk.* The group creates a grace-filled and loving structure so the person can get out of his comfort zone. Some people only value a group for its safety. They want a place where they won't be judged or condemned, and that is certainly a good thing. They want to be loved and affirmed, and we all need that.

Yet they will avoid and resist taking risks, being confronted, or doing things that make them uncomfortable. They view safety as an end, not a means to an end. It's a little like buying a car that has safety belts, bags, and alarms, yet never taking it onto the road. *Safety must serve growth; it is part of growth, not the sum of it.*

At the same time, there are people whose issues have made them so wounded and fragile that their biggest risk possible is just to show up in a group. Sometimes they will not be able to contain and handle what goes on in a group and may need to find a growth context with special expertise in their area of concern. However, those who are not so fragile, merely resistant to discomfort, can benefit by understanding that taking risk brings good things and shrinking back from risk brings little good.

God is very direct about this: "And if he shrinks back, I will not be pleased with him" (Hebrews 10:38). This is because risk is ultimately about the walk of faith, that is, stepping into what we cannot see because we trust the One who created the way. It is significant, I think, that the passage on shrinking back is followed by the best chapter in the Bible about the difficult, yet wonderful, life of faith: "Faith is being sure of what we hope for and certain of what we do not see" (Hebrews 11:1).

As members begin to take on the responsibility to be risk takers, two things happen. First, they expose weak parts to love and safety and become stronger. Second, people take more risks in more areas. They trust more, love more, "truth" more, and grow more. Risk becomes something they do every day rather than something they fear and dread. They increase capacities and desires for new experiences from God, and they truly begin to live the abundant life Jesus promised (John 10:10 NASB).

Prepare to Take Risks

Help your members accept their role as risk takers. Offer examples of risks worth taking, and decide together how to make your group a safe place for trying and failing—and risking again.

Recognize Risks Worth Taking

Here are some examples of risk areas:

- Allowing yourself to feel your emotions without editing them
- Opening up to the group with a problem you are scared of discussing
- Asking the group for help, support, or comfort
- Receiving comfort and love without running from it
- Starting off the group session yourself without waiting for someone else to do it
- Confronting someone with whom you are angry
- Asking for honest feedback about your behavior or attitude
- Asking to be held accountable for a character issue or a growth step in life outside the group

Make Risk Normal and Expected

As well, here are some tips on how to make risk normal and expected.

Talk to the members about the benefits of risk. Let them know how helpful it can be. For example, you might say, "Our group is a place where you can try new ways of relating to others, without condemnation or shame."

Help them make risk safe for each other. Show them that the safer they are, the better the group is: "Think of how much grace and safety you will need to begin taking risks, and try to provide that to every other member."

Deal with their fears. Address the reasons they haven't been able to take risks before: "Wayne, it seems you're talking about the positive parts of your life a lot. I wonder if you are concerned about what the group would think if you talked about your struggles."

Help them support risk in each other. Show them that as they become more vulnerable about experiencing different parts of themselves, it is a better group for all. "Linda, what were you feeling when

Sharon opened up? It seemed her risk taking really touched you, and she'd probably like to know about your response to her."

Your members truly benefit from a life that isn't lived so safely, but is lived by trying new ways of experiencing God, each other, and themselves.

Chapter 48

Grieve

In a certain way, it is funny to hear of a specialty group called a "grief group." Certainly we all know what the term means and why such groups exist. They are for people who are going through specific losses and need a place to process that loss. That is good and appropriate.

The funny thing is not *why* there are grief groups, but why we don't see *every* growth group as a grief group. In reality, groups must experience grief and letting go to produce life and growth! And we usually need help to go through a grief process and reach the next level of growth.

Choosing to Grieve

In the book *How People Grow*, we say that grief is different from all other pain for two reasons. First, it is a process we enter into somewhat voluntarily. We experience the losses and pain as no choice of our own. But to let go and deal with them, we have to turn our face toward the grief process. That is probably one reason why the Bible encourages us to grieve, as an act of wisdom. Solomon says,

> It is better to go to a house of mourning than to go to a house of feasting (Ecclesiastes 7:2).

> Sorrow is better than laughter, because a sad face is good for the heart. The heart of the wise is in the house of mourning, but the heart of fools is in the house of pleasure (Ecclesiastes 7:3–4).

They That Sow in Tears Will Reap in Joy

The second reason is that *grief is the pain that can heal all other pains. It is the most important pain.* When we grieve, we let go of something. We get past it. We send it away. We move on. Then whatever the *it* was can be over.

When people come to a group, for whatever reason, they will have to let go of certain things for growth to happen. But sometimes people get stuck and do not go through the process of grief, which could help them get to the next level. They deny that the loss is real, or they protest it as if it could be changed.

Take, for example, a person who is continually miserable because he cannot be "good enough." He always falls short of his expectations for himself and feels under pressure to be "better" than he is. So his chronic performance pressures trouble him. What does that have to do with grief and being stuck?

First of all, something is lost and has been denied. He has lost the approval of someone very important to him, sometimes a parent, sometimes his own ideal. He has tried and been unable to be good enough. It is a lost cause. He will never have that approval or reach that perfect, ideal self he wishes for. But instead of facing that loss, grieving it, and giving up on getting that person's approval or reaching perfection, he stays in a state of protest—as if the ideal can or should occur. So he either stays mad at the person for not giving him approval or mad at himself for not being able to get there. Either way, if he would treat it as a *lost* cause, he would get out of anger, guilt, and performance and allow himself to become sad.

Experiencing sadness would help him get better, because the sad can be comforted (Matthew 5:4). Grief can, as Solomon says, be "good for the heart." When someone gives up, gets sad, grieves something, and lets go, the heart gets happy again.

Accepting the Grief Process

When we lose something, we need to face the loss and move on. Then we can have a resurrection after the death. But to experience this resurrection, we have to move into and accept the process. The steps of this process go something like this:

- *A bad thing happens.* The loss or pain itself takes place.
- *We deny loss.* We are either too numb to really process it or just want to not believe it is true.
- *We protest.* Because we want it not to be true, we fight the reality. We bargain, perform, deal, get angry, or fight to reverse the sad truth of what has happened.
- *We enter the sadness and loss.* We give in and begin to go into the pain of sadness and grief. We say good-bye to whatever will not be and accept whatever is.
- *We reach resolution.* We accept the new reality and re-create life and ourselves around it, incorporating its new meanings and possibilities.

So whatever we lose—a person, a dream, a relationship, a career, the ideal self, Camelot, a fantasy, a wish that will never come true, someone else's approval or validation, the childhood or life we did not have— grief is part of the answer.

The Group Provides Resources to Grieve

We need resources to grieve well. These include a few things the group can provide in addition to our own decision to enter into the grief process. The members and you as facilitator all have to embrace your roles.

Each Member's Responsibility

The group should provide three things for members going through grief. We also need to experience these things for ourselves when it's our turn to enter sadness and loss.

Support. We need love, support, and comfort (Romans 12:15). We need for others to mourn with us.

Structure. We need a time, a place, and a space for grieving. We need to know the meanings of the loss and know the tasks for grieving. We need to know "how." (See *How People Grow* for a more in-depth treatment of how grieving works in the growth process.)

Process. We cannot do it in a day and must go through grief's different stages.

The Facilitator's Role

As a facilitator you have the same responsibilities as any other member to help others go through sadness and, depending on the type of group, maybe even to experience it yourself. You also have these four additional responsibilities toward your members.

Help them understand the value of letting go. Help them know that letting go is freedom, and it relates to everything from forgiveness to moving on after the loss of a relationship or a failure. Letting go is a key to spiritual growth. Help members see grief as a biblical concept that God holds dear and wants us to hold dear. If appropriate for your group, educate them in the process of denial, protest, sadness, and resolution. Information can help structure the process for them.

The group is the right place. Help them understand that the group is a place where grief and sadness are welcome. Have them talk about what makes it easier or more difficult for them to grieve and let go. Have them tell the group what they need from it.

Ask members to talk to the group about the ways they avoid grief and medicate and distract themselves. Ask the group to hold them accountable if they try to continue to do that, especially in the group. Concentrate on making your group a safe culture.

Facilitate their grief. When you see members stuck, let them know. You might comment, "I sense that you are close to sadness over that" or "It seems difficult to face that fact that you might not have her back." Such process statements help members move toward the next step.

Show them the life themes that they may not recognize as grief. Connect the dots. When they go through a loss and do not understand why it is affecting them so much, let them know. "It seems you have had a lot of losses like this. It is a theme, and I am sure that this loss taps into the others."

Hold them to their tasks. Let members know it is their role to face their losses and use each other for comfort and support. Push them toward opening up and seeing their losses for what they are and sharing them. Let them know when they are not doing it. Let them know when, as a group, they are keeping each other from the process by staying too light and cheery or spiritualizing. Confront them when they get close to grief and then change the subject, for example.

To grieve correctly is a wonderful thing. It can lead to a new life. There are few better places to do that than in a good group. But to have it happen, the members must join in. Help them to be the kind of people whom other members can grieve with, the kind who enter into the process themselves. Surely you will find God in a group that grieves.

PART 6

How to Deal with Problems in Groups

Chapter 49

Neediness

It is important to think through the problem of neediness in group members. The Bible teaches that neediness, defined as *being incomplete and without*, is something God uses to grow us up and heal us. He comes to us when we experience that we cannot fix or save ourselves in our own strength: "For he will deliver the *needy* who cry out, the afflicted who have no one to help. He will take pity on the weak and the *needy* and save the *needy* from death" (Psalm 72:12–13).

Problems in Neediness

However, neediness becomes a problem to address when it manifests in unhealthy ways, such as:

- Taking up too much group time
- Constant crises that never get resolved
- Emotional dependency that the group can't meet

- Inability to be comforted
- Not taking group advice
- Seeing the group as "not enough"

Dealing with the Core Issues of Neediness

Once you have discerned the difference between neediness that serves growth and neediness that prevents growth, you will want to understand core issues and deal with them.

Inability to connect with the group. Some needy people bring their issues to the group, but when the members reach out to them, there is a disconnect, and the needy people cannot receive the support being offered. They are unable to accept comfort and soothing. The needy person may not know how to, or may be afraid to, accept what is there for him. Make this a team issue and discuss the person's refusal or inability to value, experience, and receive the group's love and care.

Problems using the support. Sometimes a person can receive love but, for whatever reason, is unable to use the support to take growth steps. Grace and support are the "fuel" that God designed for us to metabolize—digest—and use to take responsibility for solving our problems. The person who seems to receive support but continues to stay stuck, blame, or reject help has been termed by one psychological researcher as the "help-rejecting complainer." Help the person see this: "Rob, you seem to be able to take in the connections the group is bringing to you for this issue. However, it isn't translating into decisions, action, courage, and choices for you, which is a part of the reason we use love. How can we help you with this?"

Bite-sized support. When a needy person gets into her pain or emotion, she may not be able to come out of it and may inadvertently regress to a point where she takes over the group time. Help her to use the time allotted and prepare her to mutually receive and give with the group. This often empowers the person and helps her realize she has some choices in the growth process: "Hallie, I want the group to help you with your grief and confusion. At the same time, I want the other members to get something for themselves, too. If you get into your pain tonight, is it okay if at some point I let you know we'll need to move on?" Of course, if you try this several times and she is unable to do that, you may realize the person has authentic and valid needs that may require more than the group can give.

Relational neediness versus task neediness. Sometimes people don't see that what they need is connection. Instead they go to the group for emotional rescue, looking for advice, instructions, answers, and sympathy. They need to understand that most relational supplies should make us better able to handle life's demands. While the group should certainly be a source of wisdom and truth, be aware of when members try to substitute for the attachment resource. "Natalie, often you go to the group for suggestions, but I think the members might want to give you *themselves* and see what you do with that."

A Cold Group

Be aware and monitor the group's emotional warmth and accessibility. In a group of people who live in their heads and have difficulty experiencing negative feelings, members may, without realizing it, perceive an appropriate need as excessive or bad. If you see this, confront the group's withholding and help them see that neediness is a norm for a healthy group. For example, a member who is dealing with a difficult marriage may ask for support and validation. Instead, the group may interpret his request as being too needy and therefore miss what is really going on.

Legitimate Neediness That Is Too Much for the Group

A person may suffer from an authentic, deep emptiness that requires many resources beyond what the group can provide. Sometimes it is caused by massive childhood emotional deprivation or abandonment; sometimes by a devastating loss in life. Whatever the reason, the person does need and can use comfort, safety, compassion, and structure. The problem is that the group does not possess enough of these for the person. In these situations, contact whoever is in charge of your organization and talk to them about either finding a more suitable context for the needy member or adding some supportive structure in addition to your group.

Remember that needs are a good thing. God uses them to bind us together so we can grow and heal. At the same time, develop the discernment to understand the important difference between true neediness and the fear of taking responsibility, so that you can address the person's true needs.

Chapter 50

Noncompliance

Imagine the last time you were at family dinner with young children, either your own or a friend's. If it was a casual event at home, most likely the parents said things during the meal such as, "Don't interrupt her," or "Ask for the bread; don't reach," and "Eat with your mouth closed; don't smack." It is the normal diligence of using the family meal to help kids learn about rules of life.

Recognizing Noncompliance

Group fulfills the same function as the "second family." It is a place to observe, address, and resolve noncompliance and disrespect of agreed-upon standards. Much of a group's value is in how both the noncompliant member *and* the group itself benefit from the corrective process.

Here are a few examples of noncompliance:

- Chronic lateness
- Irregular attendance

- Leaving early
- Not ending their talking when the group time is over
- Breaking confidentiality agreements during contacts with people on the outside
- Not engaging with the group during the meeting
- Constant disruption within the group (interrupting, not accepting feedback, outbursts, the equivalent of eating with your mouth open)

Deal with Root Causes

As a facilitator you should take a proactive stance toward noncompliance. Don't look at these as disruptions in the group growth. *See noncompliance as a growth issue; it is often the reason the member needs the group in the first place.* In fact, two benefits result from dealing with the problem. One is for the noncompliant member, who needs to learn to take responsibility and adapt to group norms. The other benefit is for the group, which needs to learn how to confront and deal with noncompliance with others.

Noncompliance occurs for several reasons. Identifying causes can help you deal with them.

Lack of awareness. Some group members may not know how disruptive their noncompliance is or that it is a problem in the first place. You can say, "Rachel, you're interrupting Chuck. Let's let him finish." If it is not an isolated event, but a pattern, you might say, "Rachel, it seems you interrupt people pretty often, and it looks like it affects people here. Let's talk about this."

Lack of structure. Some members may be aware of their noncompliance, but not have the internal wherewithal to modify their behavior. For example, a codependent woman may constantly come in late because she can't separate from her husband's and kids' problems or work crises. The group can help provide the structure she needs to internalize and be strengthened. They can:

- Help her deal with her fear of saying no

- Pray for her for strength and support
- Be a place where she can practice saying no to members safely
- Hold her accountable to come to group on time and deal with the anxiety
- Have her call members during the week when she is tempted to cave in
- Not allow her in after starting time and have her sit outside

Entitlement and Self-centeredness

Some people believe at heart that they shouldn't have to obey rules of conduct. This might mean they think they are entitled, deserve special treatment, or are above the rules. Others simply don't see what they are doing as affecting others, because they resist entering into another's world; things revolve around them. In this context, the leader helps the group confront the self-centered stance, yet without condemnation: "Brian, it is not your irregular attendance that is the real issue here. It is more that I don't think you think it's a big deal for us or see that it affects people. It is a big deal, and it does affect people. I want the members to tell you what it is like for them."

Rebellion and Provocation

Some members will carry into group an anti-authority agenda, in which they rebel against any norm. They will provoke you, the facilitator, and the group as being controlling authoritarians. Sometimes they will provoke people to confront them so they can dismiss the input of the group and discount them. A good approach here is to say something like, "Steve, it's hard to talk to you about your outbursts, because when we try to, you accuse us of being mean to you. We're really not, so can we look at this as your issue instead of a mean group thing? Maybe you can tell us some ways we can give you feedback that will help you take it without feeling alienated by us?"

Know your people. If a person is disruptive because of *inability and weakness*, provide as much support and help as you can. Bend over backwards to help him. Even so, if things continue, you may need to decide either to live with the problem, knowing it's the best solution, or to find a context with more structure, without shaming or judging him. If, however, the noncompliance is because of *resistance and willfulness,* keep bringing it up (1 Thessalonians 5:14). Make it a group issue and be willing to establish consequences, as we explained in chapter 29, "Confront." Finally, you may need to appeal for advice to the group ministry leader of your church or organization. Ultimately, don't sacrifice a group's growth for a member's sin.

Chapter 51

Passivity

In a group I (John) led, Robin had a problem taking charge of her life. She told us about coming from a controlling family, being raised in a legalistic church, having a domineering husband, and working for a controlling company. Over and over, the group heard her talk about how she had never been "allowed to be me."

At first the group was sympathetic and really supportive. After a while, however, they noticed that she rarely took initiative or risks, didn't make changes people suggested, and kept pointing to all the controlling people in her life. Finally, Lucy, another member, said, "Robin, are you just wanting us to take care of things for you?" Robin looked a little stunned and thought for a second. Then she said, "Yep." We all started laughing, and the group took a turn for the better.

Passivity Does Not Equal Inability

Many people are drawn to a group by a problem or situation they can't solve in their own power, such as a habit, relationship, or being stuck. Certainly we all need grace, and a group should provide abundant grace for our weaknesses, injuries, and inabilities. However, passivity is not inability. Using a baseball metaphor, *unable people keep striking out for some reason; passive people don't even take a swing.* The issue is not *can't* as much as *won't.*

Sometimes passive people will believe they are being spiritual by not doing anything. They see passivity as trusting God. This is a misunderstanding of what the Bible teaches about trusting him. Trust means having faith in God to do his tasks and taking responsibility to do what is ours: "Therefore, my dear friends, as you have always obeyed—not only in my presence, but now much more in my absence—continue to work out your salvation with fear and trembling, for it is God who works in you to will and to act according to his good purpose" (Philippians 2:12–13).

In other words, we work out things, and God works in us. It is co-laborship with God, under his direction. (For a fuller treatment of this issue, see our book *12 Christian Beliefs that Can Drive You Crazy,* chapter 4.)

Passivity is bad for the person and the group. Group should be a place where members open up, take risks, fail, learn from their failure, internalize grace and wisdom, and translate all that to their outside lives and relationships. With passivity, however, none of that happens as it should. The person does not speak up, does not confess, is not truly known by the group, stays stuck and helpless in his situation, and has few choices and options.

Why People Are Passive

Consider why people have problems with passivity, so you can help them overcome it. There is more than one cause.

Lostness. Some people have never had experience in an intimate process of any kind, and they are shell-shocked in trying to understand the rules of this new world. They may need time and safety to learn the ropes, and then they are okay.

Fear of exposure and risk. Others have learned in life that to take initiative is to be hurt, controlled, or abandoned. They have adopted a passive stance to protect themselves. Yet the protection keeps them in their prison. The group can really help people in this fix if the fearful people have willing hearts.

A hidden rescue wish. As Robin admitted, some people have a fantasy that someone will swoop down and take care of all their struggles. This is developmentally a very young condition, as it tends to be like a helpless infant's desire for her mother to totally take care of her. Such a person can benefit from a group that understands her deep desire and gradually helps her move out of the fantasy.

Help Members Overcome Passivity

A good group can do a great deal to help a passive member move beyond the problem. Here are some tips:.

See it as a problem. Help the group see that passivity doesn't solve problems; it causes them. For example, say, "Mark, when you don't open up with us, it cuts us off from you and people wonder who you really are."

Help them with their language. Passive people often use passive vocabulary, such as, "He made me . . . she wouldn't let me . . . they stopped me from. . . ." This language re-creates the problem in their heads. Bring this up, and show them how to use active (and more reality-based) language: "I allowed him to . . . I let her . . . I caved in when they. . . ." In fact, this is a helpful exercise for most group members, as it is easy to slip into passive vocabulary.

Remind and internalize. Have the group help the person by reminders, and then see if they can internalize the process. You might say, "Claudia, why don't we call on you when you are withdrawing? We'll check in with you so you can safely tell us how you are doing. And after a while, we'll see if you can volunteer on your own without our nudging." If these are safe and good experiences and the person understands the issue, this approach can work well.

Passive people are less trouble in a group than noncompliant people, but don't let them slip away. Many have terrible life problems because of their passivity, so make sure you are engaging that as an issue.

Chapter 52

Shut Up

We really don't mean to sound mean in this chapter, but we do mean this! Let's understand how the lost art of shutting up—better described as *creating room to know and be known*—is so helpful in a group context. This is a skill for you as the facilitator to learn for yourself and to pass on to the group as a norm. This issue is different from being comfortable with total group silence; it is about understanding when to talk and when to listen.

Know When to Talk

You may remember from our discussion on knowing and being known that the process takes time. It takes time to reveal, trust, and explore in order to access whatever parts of the soul need healing. When we allow people time and space, they are better able to get to whatever core issue they need to. Three elements are necessary here. The first is that caring people be present so that the person is not all alone with his feelings. The second is that the group restrain from talking when a member needs their presence without words. The third is that members who are being given feedback also know how to be quiet so they can receive what is being offered to help them.

Being quiet and listening have two great benefits. First, a member may be working on understanding and grasping an issue. Rather than filling in for him and telling him what he might be thinking, the group should allow him to struggle if he needs. Let him take ownership for figuring out what he is trying to understand. They should intervene, perhaps, if he is totally lost, but if possible, let him have his thoughts. In the same way, a member may need to experience and feel something inside that has heretofore been unsafe for him. When the group gets "talky" with him, he can easily lose a wordless experience that could be very important to his growth. Again, don't leave him twisting in the wind, so to speak, but allow him room for his feelings to emerge. Then he can process and discuss with the group. *Remember: They're his feelings, not the group's feelings.*

Although members probably think they are being caring, they often jump in too soon. This action risks not only disrupting the person's growth experience, but also not really understanding what is going on: "He who answers before listening—that is his folly and his shame" (Proverbs 18:13).

Dealing with the Talker

A related problem is that of the person who talks too much. This can be a serious issue that, left unchecked, can ruin a small group. In this situation a member's excessive talking can dominate or interrupt the processing of the group. The content can vary from person to person. It can involve his life and problems or giving advice to other members. But whatever the topic, the talker ends up controlling what is going on in the group.

When someone continues to talk too much in a group, no one is helped—neither the member nor the group. The talker is alienating himself from others, who in turn may become resentful, tune out, or leave the group: "When words are many, sin is not absent, but he who holds his tongue is wise" (Proverbs 10:19).

There are several reasons that members talk too much. Some people do not have enough internal structure and self-control. They are like a small child who simply says whatever comes to mind, having, as the saying goes, "no unexpressed thoughts." Others talk a lot to stay away from silence, as silence may cause them to feel feelings they are afraid of and want to avoid. Some want to control the perceptions others have of them, so talking gives them a sense that they are being seen as a good person. Others can be needy inside and talk in hopes that others will take care of them. Some take on a parental role, giving unwanted advice to others in the group. And others have a form of narcissism (see chapter 54) that manifests itself in talking about themselves in self-absorption that ignores the feelings and concerns of others.

Whatever the cause, good groups should deal with over-talking. Most likely, whatever negative reactions the talker is creating in the group, she is also creating in her outside life. The group can help this situation at very meaningful levels. Here are some ways to deal with the over-talkative member:

Begin with the event, not the issue. In the beginning, address the problem as it relates to a group interaction: "Beth, hold on, I want to hear what Glenn is saying," or "Jeff, let's let someone else have the floor now." Sometimes that will be enough of a nudge to help remind the talker not to overdo it, especially if he cares about how he affects people.

Help him become aware. The talker may not know that he dominates the group. It may simply be something he has not been told directly. Let him know what happens: "I don't know if you are aware of it, Jen, but a couple of times tonight you've cut Teresa off and she sort of withdrew. Can we explore that with you?" or "Keith, sometimes it's hard for other people to connect when you talk a lot. Let's address what is going on with this."

Bring the group in. Member's responses can help the talker. The community, not just the facilitator, gives the feedback and support, which is deeper and more powerful: "Brian, you look like you went away when Stephanie started talking. What went on?" or "Linda, I wonder if you have any feelings about what happened when Melanie changed the subject to herself."

Let the group generate the feedback. As we have shown in other scenarios, the most effective intervention is when the group creates the feedback while the facilitator more or less sets up the confrontation: "What's going on right now?" or "It seems the tone of the group has just changed. Does anyone have any idea why?"

Set limits to help the person. Sometimes a talker will benefit from a consequence that helps remind him to restrain himself. The group can humorously say something to him if he goes overboard, like "gong!" or "time!" In time, however, this function should be internalized by the member and should be discontinued once he has the self-control.

Do not be afraid of confronting the talker with grace and truth. It is easy to avoid this, thinking she needs the extra time. On occasion she might, as most everyone does. However, if it is a pattern and you see that the group is reacting, no one is being helped by ignoring it. Much can be gained by bringing up the problem.

Chapter 53

Aggression

Imagine for a moment that you are being invited to sign up for a group and the leader is telling you all the benefits you can expect: growth, togetherness, community, learning, wisdom, fun, spiritual development, and the like. Joining the group sounds so good, you just can't wait for it to start. All those things are what you have been seeking for so long. You say, "Yes, for sure."

Prepare to Be Proactive

Now imagine that the leader also says, "You can expect to get those benefits in very small doses, because there is going to be one person who is really aggressive and pushy. He asserts his opinions all the time and tends to run over people and control the group process. And since I am a really nice group leader, I don't want to make waves. So I won't be saying anything to stop that, and you will have to try really hard to work around it and find some crumbs of that growth I talked about. It will be great. Look forward to seeing you. Bring the doughnuts."

Do you think you might feel different as you look forward to the group? Of course you do. But aggressive members are the reality for a lot of groups. Leaders don't warn you, but it happens. The well-intentioned group leader lets the pushy person ruin much of the group experience for everyone else. And the members feel disillusioned meeting after meeting, slowly losing interest in the group itself.

We would like you to take a proactive stance toward this problem before it begins. See yourself in the way that we have talked about all along: *the guardian of the process.* You are the advocate for the group members, and if they are suffering under the pushy person's control, then they need you to protect the group purpose.

Choose Appropriate Interventions

Make sure you use the level of intervention appropriate for the group. The least level is directing traffic, and the deepest is the full-blown processing of the issue in the group. Your intervention depends on the group's purpose, agreements, expectations, and openness.

Be Direct But Not Disruptive

Use your gut to know how others are feeling. If it is bothering you, let that be a sign that others might feel the same way. Don't sit and suffer too long, because you are probably losing people. However, make sure that you are balanced in this issue, too. If it is your pet peeve, you may need to seek balance. If needed, talk to someone about what you are doing.

The least disruptive, least intrusive intervention is to take control directly, but without making process comments or confrontation. Again, the appropriateness of the group purpose and the ground rules enter in. If you are not confronting each other as part of the group, then just facilitate. You might say:

- "Hold on for a second, Joe. I want to hear the rest of what Susie was saying."
- "Thanks, Joe, but we haven't heard from some others yet. I want to make sure we hear from everyone in the group."

- "Hang on, Joe. I think that kind of advice might be past the ground rules that we set up. Why don't you just hold on to that?"

In other words, don't make an issue of what is happening. You are something like a policeman in the intersection of a traffic jam, making sure things keep flowing.

Confront outside the Group

The next level would be confronting the aggressive person outside the group. Give Joe feedback in a way that does not become part of the group itself. If the group has not chosen process and feedback and Joe is becoming disruptive, take Joe aside. You might say:

- "Joe, I would like to make you aware of something. You have a lot of ideas and are very verbal, and I appreciate your wanting to contribute. I need for you to watch how much you say, however. Some of the other people are not getting a chance to talk. Could you be aware of that for me?"
- "Joe, I am concerned that you are giving some advice where people are not desiring it. We talked about this being a place where we would not do that, and you are doing it. I am afraid that it might make some people uncomfortable with sharing. So please hold off on that. Thanks."
- "Joe, are you aware of the amount of input you give compared with the other members? I didn't think you were, just because you are a verbal person. Try to watch that and see if you can help me make the sharing time more evenly divided. I want everyone to get a chance."

Deal with It within the Group

You can deal with the issue in the group, if that is part of the covenant. It would sound much like the above, but in the context of the meeting. You could ask others if they had noticed Joe's action and ask them to give Joe feedback. Also, you could have them talk about what it is like for them, what their experience is. Again, this has to be something the group has agreed to.

Finally, if you are in a very process-oriented group, you could make it a group process issue and deal with it that way. "Is anyone noticing what just happened?" When Joe interrupts, you can have them deal with it and go from there. Another way is to say, "I notice that something happens here a lot. Someone is talking and Joe kind of takes over. Then the person—in this case, Susie—shuts down, and no one ever brings it up. Does anyone else notice that? What is going on there? Why hasn't anyone said anything?"

Remember that you are to model grace and truth and follow the rules for confrontation mentioned earlier, especially in chapter 15. And make sure you have others do that as well.

No one likes to have a group dominated by someone. Remember, you are the leader, and it is your job to protect the group from that dynamic. You don't have to do it deeply, but you have to do it if things are going to work well. Get some support if needed, but keep order. Otherwise, you will lose people.

Chapter 54

Narcissism

If you are a sixth grader, you know this problem. You don't use the term *narcissism,* but you still know the problem. You say things like "Sally thinks she is cooler than everyone else" and "Marty always brags" and "Susie thinks she knows everything." You find a thousand ways to describe the problem of people who think they are somehow ideal, better than the rest, perfect, without flaws or problems, or have it all together.

On a playground you can avoid the person. In a friendship or other relationship, you can sometimes work around or even enjoy the narcissism. Narcissistic people can have other parts to them that are very lovable; we are not trying to suggest they are all bad. In reality, all of us have some degree of narcissism. It is part of the human condition to want to be more ideal than we are. So in most situations we enjoy narcissism, work with it, tolerate it, avoid it, or find some way to live with it.

Narcissism Affects the Group

In a group, however, narcissism can be somewhat problematic. If someone thinks he is superior, without issues or problems, or wants all the attention, his narcissism affects the group process. The same is true when a member wishes to be ideal or be seen as ideal by the group. Since it's important that people be their "real selves" for groups to flourish, you can see the problem. Narcissism is designed to hide our real selves because of shame and other problems. So it works directly against being real.

Also, another type of narcissism is caused not by shame, but by pride, arrogance, and omnipotence. Since growth takes place only in the context of humility, you can see a further problem. If people aren't really trying to feel superior to cover up shame and crummy feelings about themselves, but actually believe they *are* better, growth is very difficult to achieve. This holds true for anyone who assumes a godlike stance as a primary identity. And those in the wake of an arrogant narcissist do not tend to fare well, because narcissists don't understand vulnerability.

This arrogance creates another problem for a group indeed. The arrogant person may try to take over and become the "god" of the group, the "god-keeper" for the group, or the spokesperson for God. Ugly!

Guard the Group

However you deal with it, it is important to be aware of narcissism. Generally, the fix is somewhat like the one for aggression. You move from controlling traffic to trying to work it through, individually or with the group. It all depends on the group's appropriateness, agenda, and purpose.

Set the Tone

Talk about the human pressure to look as if we have it all together and impress each other. Make "searching for the ideal self" a topic of discussion. Talk about how we cover shame and crummy feelings about ourselves by trying to appear better than we are. Ask if members can relate to that. What shame might they be covering?

Again, talk about the culture you want to have, one where people are real and humble in the ways we discussed earlier. Ask the group how that is going and how you might have more of it. Make it an ongoing part of your cultural talks and discussions.

Be Direct But Not Disruptive

Again, check your gut to know how others are feeling. As with aggression, if narcissism is bothering you, it is probably getting to others. So don't let the narcissist dominate the group with being so wonderful for too long. Do something, unless the problem is so benign it does not bother people and you have decided that this is not the place to deal with it. But at least stay aware.

The least disruptive, least intrusive intervention is just to take control directly, but without making process comments or confrontation. Again, the appropriateness of the group purpose and the ground rules enter in here. If you are not confronting each other as part of the group, then just facilitate.

- "I know, Joe, that you don't feel those sorts of struggles. But some do, and I want to hear about Sue's before we go on."
- "Thanks, Joe, but it is not that great for everyone. How do some of the rest of you feel?"
- "Hang on, Joe. I think that kind of advice might be past the ground rules we set up. Why don't you just hold on to that?"

So narcissism is not something to be talked about, just contained.

Address It outside the Group

The next level would be a confrontation from you outside the group. It would involve giving Joe some feedback in a way that does not become a part of the group itself. If the group is not one where process and feedback are happening, and Joe is becoming disruptive, take Joe aside one night and just give him some feedback.

- "Joe, I would like to make you aware of something. It seems that every time you share, it is about how great you are doing or how wonderful things are for you. I am afraid that might be making others feel less likely to share struggles."

- "Joe, I am concerned that you are a little unaware of the other people in the group sometimes and how you might make them feel. Do you know that you come across a little 'higher' or 'better' than everyone else? Kind of like you don't struggle with the same things that others do? Is that how you really feel?"
- "Joe, are you aware of the amount of sharing you do compared with the other members? I didn't think you were, just because you are a verbal person. Try to watch that and see if you can help me make the sharing time more evenly divided. I want everyone to get a chance."

Address Narcissism within the Group

If addressing issues is part of the covenant, then address this problem within the group. Follow the same procedure you would with aggression or another issue. You could ask others if they notice the dynamic of narcissism and whether they have feedback for Joe. Also, you could have them talk about what it is like for them, what their experience is to be with him and hear him. Again, this has to be something the group has agreed to want.

Finally, with a very process-oriented group that really wants to get into things, you could make it a group issue. "Is anyone noticing what just happened?" When Joe talks, you can have them deal with it and go from there. Another way is to say, "I notice that something happens here a lot. Sometimes when Joe shares, everyone kind of drops out. Things change in the group, but no one ever really talks about it. What is going on there? Does anyone notice this? What are you feeling when that happens?"

Be sure to model grace and truth, and follow the rules for confrontation that we mentioned earlier. And make sure that you have others do that as well.

Remember the rule again: *Guard the process.* If you are struggling with the person, so are others. Check in with the appropriate intervention, and be an advocate for the group. If it is not right to confront or make it an issue or process it in the group, then contain it. Figure out the right level, and do something. The process depends on it.

Chapter 55

Spiritualization

After doing years of groups, we heard group members using "spiritual" sayings that had little to do with the Bible—and everything to do with keeping them from growth and process. In fact, as we analyzed the sayings, we saw that people often said such things *to keep others from feeling what they were feeling and processing what they were processing.* The sayings were mostly to avoid pain and issues that the "listener" did not know what to do with.

Because of that, we wrote a book entitled *12 "Christian" Beliefs That Can Drive You Crazy.*

Define the Problem

Most people are familiar with the term *spiritualize.* While it has different meanings for different people, it mostly means to *give lofty spiritual explanation or input that is no more than an unhelpful, pat answer.* It avoids the real issue at hand. Job's friends were spiritualizers. They tried to tell him what was wrong with him and how to get better instead of just loving him through his process of pain, loss, and trauma. Maybe you have experienced your own versions of that dynamic.

The long and the short of spiritualization is that it does two unhelpful things. First, it stops a person from going through the experience. For example, it's common for a person going through pain to get spiritualized advice. A well-meaning person will quote Romans 8:28 and say, "Don't feel bad. God makes all things work out for the good." Certainly that is true, but for the suffering person, it is also true that whatever has happened might not be good at all and is extremely painful. Another common example is when a death occurs and the grieving person hears, "Don't be sad. Your (loved one) is in heaven now." That timing of giving hope may stop the grief process.

So the process is stopped and the person in pain or struggle takes her heart away from the other person (or the group) and is now, from a heart perspective, in it all alone. She might smile on the outside, even sing hymns. But on the inside she is alone with the pain.

Second, spiritualization often misses the real biblical truth that would apply to the person and his pain at that moment. The "God answer" is not at all God's answer for that moment. For instance, the proper verse for the moment might be "mourn with those who mourn" (Romans 12:15). The person who is grieving may not need to be encouraged at that moment, but to be connected within his grief.

There is no way to list all the possible ways to spiritualize. The book we mentioned above makes a pretty good start. But even though we cannot list all the forms of spiritualization here, be careful of the main dynamic and know that it is the use of "spiritual language" to avoid dealing with pain or life. It is a way of bailing out of the process. And when we do that, we also cut the person off from experiencing God in the depth of her problem. We shut the door.

Monitor the Balance

While spiritual input is important, and while we desire the proper use of Scripture, be careful with it. Monitor it in your group. Finding out God's ways is an important element of our ministry of reconciliation. We want people to know what the Bible says about life and learn how to implement his ways. But don't use Scripture and spiritual truths to keep people from experiencing biblical truth. That's what the Pharisees did.

Evaluate the Language

Evaluate someone's "God talk" or "Scripture talk" to figure out its effect. While we cannot often understand the intent of the one who uses it, we can see what it does to the hearer or the process. Does it shut the person down? Does it help her feel loved? Does it give a timely truth or correction, or does it punish? Look at the fruit of the saying in the moment. Realize that some of the talk about God and the Bible was not helpful *at the time it was given, but could be helpful later, even moments later.* A lot of what is said is good; it is just not the right time. Intervene and say, "Joe, that is helpful to hear. Let's wait a little while and then share it. I want to hear more of what Susie is experiencing and thinks."

Get the Group's Perspective

Ask the members how they feel in terms of whether the group is real enough or is at times becoming more "religious" than "spiritual." Ask if they think there are more platitudes given than looking at real life.

Intervene Appropriately

If one person tends to spiritualize, decide what kind of intervention is appropriate. Use the guides in the chapters on aggression (53) and narcissism (54) for how to go from light to more process interventions. You can address the problem inside or outside the group, depending on what is appropriate.

If you see that spiritualizing has become a dynamic of the whole group, not just one person, then talk to the group. Try to move them past it. Ask if they can tell the difference between spiritual content and spiritualizing. Watch for how engaged people are. Notice the process and how it is doing. Sometimes people nod and agree to spiritual talk, only to shut down afterward. If you notice that this has happened, address it appropriately.

It's tricky to maintain a balance in a Christian group between good use of Scripture or God language and process. But the Bible is a book about real life, and when it is used to avoid real life, we are no longer doing what it says. As the leader, have your group be in reality and have their talk about God and the Bible be real as well.

Go and Grow

We hope that you have found the material in this book helpful for your situation. This book has been especially meaningful to us because of all the people like you with whom we have been in contact over the years. We have worked with group facilitators, both experienced and new, who love God, who desire to see people find growth and healing in his paths, and who value the small group experience as a means for that to happen.

Thank you for your heart, your passion, and your involvement in the group process, and may God bless your efforts.

"From him the whole body, joined and held together by every supporting ligament, grows and builds itself up in love, as each part does its work" (Ephesians 4:16).

Getting More Out of This Book

Making Small Groups Work equips small group leaders with the "how-tos" of leading a small group. It was designed not only to help you create the right environment for growth, but also to give the practical tools needed to make your group one that truly impacts lives. No matter what "kind" of group you lead, these processes and information go a long way in helping you accomplish your goal of having a group that really works.

In addition to the facilitation skills the leader brings to the group, there is another very important ingredient for a successful group: the selection of materials or curriculum to use. The materials you choose for group study are often as important as the skills you gain and the environment you create. It is a matter to be considered very carefully by you, the group or ministry leader, as you play a key role in helping others down God's path.

Over the last decade, Drs. John Townsend and Henry Cloud have created an abundance of small group materials that promote overall spiritual growth within specific life contexts—such as marriage, dating, or parenting—and that help solve specific life problems. They have also created materials that help you build a bridge between your spiritual life and your real life and give you the tools to overcome the obstacles that keep all of us from experiencing the full life God intends.

The most powerful groups impart two kinds of learning: content and process. The Cloud-Townsend small group materials are designed to achieve a balance between imparting practical knowledge about each content area and giving the group a structured process that helps the members experience what they need to experience with each other in order to grow.

Each of the books described below is a part of a system of spiritual maturity, emotional growth, and character development. They contain powerful biblical principles that offer practical solutions for the difficulties we all face in our day-to-day lives. This material will help you grow closer to God, make better decisions, find personal fulfillment, and improve all kinds of relationships. All of these materials are offered in a format conducive to a small group setting. Many of these books are available in a video format with a leader's guide and participant's guide. Companion workbooks are also available.

We hope the following small group resources will guide you as you select materials for your groups. May God bless you as you make your own small group work in a way that impacts lives!

How People Grow
by Dr. Henry Cloud
and Dr. John Townsend

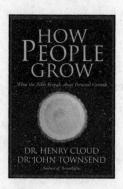

This book addresses what the Bible says about personal and spiritual growth. It helps you understand the growth process according to God's plan for our lives. It talks about what has to happen for growth to occur and about the tough questions many of us have asked at one time or another: Does Christianity really work? Why do so many sincere Christians fail to make progress in a particular area of their life?

The book explores what the Bible teaches about the responsibilities of the church and the responsibilities of the individual. It gives pastors, recovery leaders, lay leaders, and paraprofessionals tools to help people resolve issues of relationships, maturity, emotional problems, and overall spiritual growth. It includes tips for group facilitators and group members.

The authors examine the processes that actually help people grow and made a discovery: The true processes that make people grow are all in the Bible. Not only is the Bible true, but what is true is in the Bible. The problem, they contend, is that many systems of growth leave out much of what the Bible teaches.

In this foundational work Drs. Cloud and Townsend describe the principles they use in their private practice, their teaching and seminars, and their other books. Their practical approach to helping people grow really works and has transforming power in people's lives because their principles are grounded in both orthodox Christian faith and a keen understanding of human nature. This book will be useful both to those who are helping people grow spiritually as well as to those who are seeking growth themselves.

Changes That Heal

by Dr. Henry Cloud

Christians suffer from a whole range of emotional problems: anxiety, loneliness, grief over broken relationships, resentment, and feelings of inadequacy. *Changes That Heal* teaches that biblical solutions for these struggles lie in understanding certain basic developmental tasks. These tasks involve growing up into the "likeness" of the God who created us.

In this book Dr. Cloud takes the reader step by step through the four basic tasks of becoming mature adults. He identifies four aspects of the personality of God that, if we cultivate them, will greatly improve our day-to-day functioning.

1. Bond with others
2. Separate from others
3. Sort out issues of good and bad
4. Take charge as an adult

Changes That Heal is the vital first step in the process of spiritual maturity and emotional growth. Understanding these four tasks is essential to all fulfilling relationships.

Hiding from Love
by Dr. John Townsend

Many of us hide from the things we long for most—from connection, intimacy, and love. When you experience emotional injury, fear, or shame, your first impulse is to hide the hurting parts of yourself from God, others, and even yourself. Often you have learned these hiding patterns during childhood to protect yourself in a threatening environment; however, when you hide your injuries and frailties, you isolate yourself from the very things you need to heal and mature. What served as protection for a child becomes a prison to an adult.

In *Hiding from Love*, Dr. John Townsend helps you thoroughly explore the hiding pattern you've developed and guides you toward the healing grace and truth God has built into safe, connected relationships with himself and others. This book leads you toward healing and a new freedom and joy in living.

Boundaries
by Dr. Cloud and Dr. Townsend

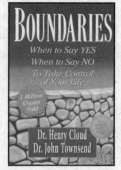

This Gold Medallion Award-winning book presents a biblical treatment of boundaries, how they are developed and how they become injured. It shows the common misconceptions of the function and purpose of boundaries and how to develop and maintain healthy limits while loving. It addresses specific issues that confront today's Christians, such as the following:

- Living a life out of control
- Having people take advantage of us
- Having trouble saying no
- Being disappointed with God because of unanswered prayers
- Setting limits and still being loving

- Dealing with people upset or hurt by our boundaries
- Feeling guilty or afraid when we consider setting boundaries

Having clear boundaries is essential to a healthy, balanced lifestyle. Often Christians focus so much on being loving and unselfish that they forget their own limits and limitations. Boundaries impact all areas of life. Physical boundaries help us determine who may touch us, mental boundaries give us the freedom to have our own thoughts, emotional boundaries help us to deal with our own emotions, and spiritual boundaries help us distinguish God's will from our own.

Safe People
by Dr. Cloud and Dr. Townsend

Too many of us have invested ourselves in relationships where we have been taken advantage of or that have left us feeling deeply wounded or abandoned. If you're one who has chosen the wrong people to get involved with or makes the same mistakes in relationships over and over again, *Safe People* offers you a remedy.

This book gives solid guidance to help you do the following:

- Correct things within yourself that jeopardize your relational security
- Learn the twenty traits of "unsafe" people
- Recognize what makes people trustworthy
- Avoid unhealthy relationships
- Form positive relationships

In *Safe People,* Drs. Cloud and Townsend offer solid guidance for making safe choices in relationships, from friendships to romance. They help us identify the nurturing people we all need in our lives as well as the unhealthy ones we need to avoid.

12 "Christian" Beliefs That Can Drive You Crazy
by Dr. Cloud and Dr. Townsend

This book identifies twelve teachings that sound plausible because they each contain a nugget of truth. However, when a Christian tries to apply these concepts, a breakdown occurs and the person needlessly suffers. This book explores these common false assumptions that people develop from either misreading the Bible or listening to someone teach who misinterprets God's truth. Most of these have one thing in common: They draw believers away from God's resources of growth and healing, and toward a system that sounds Christian, but doesn't work. Drs. Cloud and Townsend believe the Bible can help make you emotionally well. God and his Word are part of the solution, not part of the problem.

In this book you are able to identify the pseudo-biblical beliefs that can make you crazy. You learn how to apply the truth of God's Word, his Spirit, and his people to grow in grace and in truth.

The Mom Factor
by Dr. Cloud and Dr. Townsend

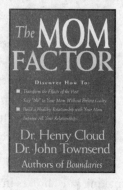

No one has influenced the person you are today as much as your mother has. The way Mom handled your needs as a child has shaped your worldview, your relationships, your marriage, your career, your self-image, and your life. *The Mom Factor* steers you down a path of discovery and growth beyond the effects of six common mothering styles.

- The Phantom Mom
- The China Doll Mom
- The Controlling Mom
- The Trophy Mom

- The Still-the-Boss Mom
- The American Express Mom

In this book you will find a hopeful, realistic, and empowering approach to identifying your unmet mothering needs and filling them in healthy, life-changing ways through other people. This encouraging book doesn't just help you understand areas in your life that need change and strengthening; it also helps you apply your discoveries to attain new freedom and joy in living and an increased ability to give and receive love. And it gives you a new, healthier way of relating to your mother today.

Boundaries in Dating
by Dr. Cloud and Dr. Townsend

Boundaries in Dating helps readers of all ages to avoid the pitfalls of dating. It provides structure for the dating process and helps singles to think, solve problems, and enjoy the benefits of dating to the hilt, increasing their abilities to find and commit to a marriage partner. This practical book is filled with insightful, true-life examples and includes such topics as

- Sins You Can Live With—Recognizing and choosing quality over "perfection" in a dating partner
- Don't Fall in Love with Someone You Wouldn't Be Friends With—How to ensure that honest friendship is one vital component in a relationship
- Don't Screw Up a Friendship Out of Loneliness—Preserving friendships by separating between platonic relationships and romantic interest
- Kiss False Hope Good-Bye—Moving past denial to deal with real relational problems in a realistic and hopeful way

Boundaries in Dating reveals a wise biblical path to developing self-control, freedom, and intimacy in the dating process. It will help you experience dating as a fun and rewarding experience.

Boundaries in Marriage
by Dr. Cloud and Dr. Townsend

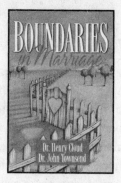

This book shows couples how to apply important boundary principles to building a strong marriage in which "two become one" without compromising their individual integrity, freedom, or truth. How do you work out conflict, establish healthy communication, solve problems and deal with differing needs?

You learn how to apply the principles of the Gold Medallion Award-winning book *Boundaries*. This book helps couples experience marriage at its best, as a haven for mutual love, care, appreciation, and growth. Drs. Cloud and Townsend show why true, joyous unity in marriage requires that both partners define and maintain their integrity as well as respect their mate's personal boundaries.

Boundaries in Marriage shows couples

- Why boundaries are very important for a thriving productive marriage
- How values form the structure of a marriage
- How to protect a marriage from intruders, whether parents, other people, affairs, or personal idols
- Why each partner needs to establish personal boundaries and how this is done
- How to work with a spouse who understands values and boundaries and how to work with one who doesn't

Using principles from the Bible, *Boundaries in Marriage* can help both new and seasoned couples protect their marriage and make even the best marriage better.

Boundaries with Kids
by Dr. Cloud and Dr. Townsend

Helping children learn responsibility is a key issue for anyone in a parenting or teaching role. From temper tantrums and attitude problems to drugs and sex, learning limits and becoming responsible is a major part of growing up. Kids who haven't learned these skills often struggle in many important areas, such as relationships, school, conduct, work, spirituality, and morality.

As any parent knows, simply telling kids to "do the right thing" isn't enough. And "making them mind" is often futile. *Boundaries with Kids* helps grown-ups teach children how to become stewards of their lives, behavior, and values by establishing healthy boundaries with them. As parents learn to set appropriate boundaries and consequences with children, the kids begin developing

- Ownership of their lives
- Discipline and self-control
- Respect for others
- Love and freedom

The book is based on some of the same biblical principles found in the best-selling *Boundaries* and is appropriate for kids of all ages, from birth to eighteen. *Boundaries with Kids* will help your child learn responsibility by teaching you how to

- Recognize the boundary issues underlying child behavior problems
- Set boundaries and appropriate consequences with kids
- Get out of the "nagging" trap
- Stop controlling your child and start helping your child develop self-control
- Apply the ten laws of boundaries to parenting
- Take six practical steps for implementing boundaries with your kids

Raising Great Kids
by Dr. Cloud and Dr. Townsend

Parenting is a complex and demanding task—and one of the most important responsibilities any person ever takes on. The responsibility of someone's life in your hands, given your own failings, can make anyone anxious and unsure. Child rearing is the job of nurturing and training a child over time into someone who is ready for adulthood. This takes time, love, and effort.

This book takes the approach that the job of parenting is primarily that of developing character in the child. Character is the sum of a child's abilities to deal with life as God intended. There are six important traits of character that parents need to develop in children at all ages and stages of development.

- Connectedness—Learning to relate, trust, and attach to God and safe people
- Responsibility—Taking ownership of their lives, behavior, emotions, and values
- Reality—Learning to deal with imperfect people in an imperfect world (including themselves)
- Competence—Developing skills and expertise in school, tasks, jobs, and other areas
- Morality—Becoming a person with a healthy conscience and ethics
- Worship/spiritual life—Developing a vital and ongoing relationship with God

As parents apply themselves to these areas of character, children learn to function with the many demands that life puts on them. In addition, *Raising Great Kids* addresses the important issue of balancing love and discipline, a confusing area for many parents. The book provides principles to help parents remain in control of the parenting process.

Raising Great Kids apples to kids of all ages, from birth to eighteen, and will provide parents with a biblical and practical way to successfully conduct the child-rearing process with grace and truth.

God Will Make a Way
by Dr. Cloud and Dr. Townsend

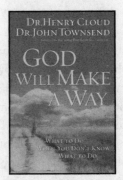

God Will Make a Way presents eight guiding principles by which we are to live. Life for every person on earth is a challenging journey, with or without God. Those who invite God to join them on this adventure believe that when bad things happen, they can trust God to be present and work on their behalf. Drs. Cloud and Townsend believe God has given us instructions on how he makes a way for us when we call on him. When you pursue the following eight principles, you can thrive relationally, emotionally, and spiritually. These principles offer a new approach to recognize when God is present and how he works his will in our lives. The Principles of the Way:

- Begin your journey with God
- Choose your travel companions wisely
- Place high value on wisdom
- Leave your baggage behind
- Own your faults and weaknesses
- Embrace problems as gifts
- Take life as it comes
- Love God with all you are

God Will Make a Way shows the principles at work in twelve key areas of life: dating, marriage, sex, conflict, parenting, fear, lost love, addiction, anger, depression, weight loss, and personal goals. It is a practical and helpful book presenting a life system that reveals God's wisdom for coping with our most difficult problems.

For more details on these small group materials, please visit the website *www.cloudtownsend.com*

How to Have That Difficult Conversation You've Been Avoiding

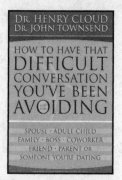

by Dr. Cloud and Dr. Townsend

Successful people confront well. They know that setting healthy boundaries improves relationships. They have discovered that uncomfortable—even dangerous—situations can often be avoided or resolved through direct conversation. But most of us don't know how to go about having difficult conversations. We see confrontation as scary or adversarial. We're afraid to ask a boss for a raise or talk to a relative about a drinking problem, or even address a relational conflict with a spouse or someone we are dating.

In *How to Have That Difficult Conversation You've Been Avoiding,* Cloud and Townsend take the principles from their bestselling book *Boundaries* and apply them to a variety of the most common difficult situations and relationships.

- Explains why confrontation is essential in all arenas of life
- Shows how healthy confrontation can improve relationships
- Presents the essentials of a good boundary-setting conversation
- Provides tips on how to prepare for the conversation
- Shows how to tell people what you want, how to stop bad behavior, and how to deal with counterattack
- Gives actual sample conversations to have with your spouse, date, kids, coworker, boss, parents, and more

Special Training Series with Dr. Henry Cloud—
Live via Satellite on CCN!

Equip your small group leaders—and members—with a fresh vision for transforming small groups into growth groups.

Groups That Grow:
Your People and Your Church
with Dr. Henry Cloud

Live via satellite on CCN

Topics include

Growth group basics
How to build connection in a group
Confrontation in the small group setting
The evolution of the small group leader

... and more

For more information, call 800-321-6781 or visit www.ccnonline.net

Embark on a
Life-Changing Journey
of Personal and Spiritual Growth

DR. HENRY CLOUD   DR. JOHN TOWNSEND

Dr. Henry Cloud and Dr. John Townsend have been bringing hope and healing to millions for over two decades. They have helped people everywhere discover solutions to life's most difficult personal and relational challenges. Their material provides solid, practical answers and offers guidance in the areas of *parenting, singles issues, personal growth,* and *leadership.*

Bring either Dr. Cloud or Dr. Townsend to your church or organization. They are available for:

- Seminars on a wide variety of topics
- Training for small group leaders
- Conferences
- Educational events
- Consulting with your organization

Other opportunities to experience Dr. Cloud and Dr. Townsend:

- Ultimate Leadership workshops—held in Southern California throughout the year.
- Small group curriculum
- Seminars via Satellite
- Solutions Audio Club—Solutions is a weekly recorded presentation

For other resources, and for dates of seminars and workshops
by Dr. Cloud and Dr. Townsend, visit:
www.cloudtownsend.com

For other information **Call (800) 676-HOPE (4673)**

Or write to:
Cloud-Townsend Resources
3176 Pullman Street, Suite 105
Costa Mesa, CA

We want to hear from you. Please send your comments about this book to us in care of zreview@zondervan.com. Thank you.